The WITCH and WIZARD SPELLBOOK

Empowering Your Life with Natural Magic (Alpha Books, 2004)

Empowering Your Life with Dreams (Alpha Books, 2003)

Empowering Your Life with Wicca (Alpha Books, 2003)

Wiccan Spell A Day (Kensington/Citadel, 2002)

The Book of Reincarnation (Barron's, 2002)

The Cyber Spellbook (New Page Books, 2002)

Goddess Bless! (Red Wheel, 2002)

Faery Magic (New Page Books, 2002)

The Wiccan Spell Kit (Kensington/Citadel, 2001)

A Witch Like Me (New Page Books, 2001)

The Wiccan Web (Kensington/Citadel, 2001)

The Witch and Wizard Training Guide (Kensington/Citadel, 2001)

Exploring Celtic Druidism (New Page Books, 2001)

Dream Magic (HarperSanFrancisco, 2000)

Celtic Traditions (Kensington/Citadel, 2000)

The Little Giant Encyclopedia of Runes (Sterling, 2000)

Love, Sex, and Magic (Kensington/Citadel, 1999)

The Shapeshifter Tarot (Llewellyn, 1998)

The Pocket Guide to Celtic Spirituality (Crossing Press, 1998)

The Pocket Guide to Crystals and Gemstones (Crossing Press, 1998)

Moonflower: Erotic Dreaming with the Goddess (Llewellyn, 1996)

Greenfire: Making Love with the Goddess (Llewellyn, 1995)

THE WITCH AND WIZARD SPELLBOOK

SIRONA KNIGHT

CITADEL PRESS
Kensington Publishing Corp.
www.kensingtonbooks.com

Note: The improper use of essential oils and herbs is potentially dangerous. Certain people may be sensitive or have an allergic reaction to some product ingredients. Please consult your health care professional. Neither the publisher nor the author can be held responsible for any adverse effects or consequences resulting from the use of any of the charms or spells in this book.

CITADEL PRESS BOOKS are published by

Kensington Publishing Corp.
850 Third Avenue
New York, NY 10022

All Kensington titles, imprints, and distributed lines are available at special quantity discounts for bulk purchases for sales promotions, premiums, fund-raising, educational, or institutional use. Special book excerpts or customized printings can also be created to fit specific needs. For details, write or phone the office of the Kensington special sales manager: Kensington Publishing Corp., 850 Third Avenue, New York, NY 10022, attn: Special Sales Department; phone 1-800-221-2647.

CITADEL PRESS and the Citadel logo are Reg. U.S. Pat. & TM Off.

First printing: June 2005

10 9 8 7 6 5 4 3 2 1

Printed in the United States of America

Library of Congress Control Number: 2004099325

ISBN 0-8065-2684-X

This book is dedicated
to all of you who love the
Harry Potter books by J. K. Rowling
as much as I do!
Blessed be!

Where Are They Now?

ROBERT F. POTTS

Where are they now, those faerie folk
Who once dwelt in my wood
When I was young, who played with me
And taught me what they could?
I'd hear the Dryad sing her song
In the shadows by a twisting stream.
I'd chase the elves and they'd chase me.
I'd hide behind a magic tree
Or in a moonlight beam.

Where did they go? When did they leave?
I can't recall the day.
Did I say goodbye to them
And watch them go away?
Or did I just forget to look
One day when I was older?
Did I, perhaps, just slip astray,
Neglect to go one winter day,
A world-wise youth and getting colder?

I'll go back now to the wood
Again to find the grace,
The long-missed fun of tiny folk,
Of meeting faeries face to face.
I will find them and I'll stay this time.
I'll not again forget their names.
I'm younger now, not near so wise
As when I wore a young man's guise.
It's time I joined their games.

CONTENTS

INTRODUCTION

THE TREMENDOUS SUCCESS of J. K. Rowling's Harry Potter series and J. R. R. Tolkien's *The Lord of the Rings* (and the movies made from them too) shows that magic still lives in our hearts, minds, and imaginations. Now the magic is growing stronger as more people realize and remember who they truly are.

The art and craft of magic is all about fulfilling your potential and becoming the person you want to be. Once you learn the basic techniques, you can personalize them to fit your lifestyle. That is the beauty of magical traditions—they are made to be part of your life rather than expecting you to adhere and conform to an outside set of codes of regulations.

Traditionally, magic came from divine places, and when humans tapped into that divine energy, extraordinary things happened. I recently received an e-mail in which a person described how his father had an almost fatal stroke one day, but the next day he was sitting up in his hospital bed, talking about how he had been healed in a dream by an angel of light. Events like these always make me realize yet again that there are extraordinary powers afoot. The unknown, waiting to become known, the unmanifested waiting to be manifested, this is what people call magic. But magic is actually all of us realizing our true, divine potential.

I know this to be true because I have experienced events in my life that defy the bounds of normal perception. I shape shift, I experience past lives, and I enter a world of magic that has been practiced since the dawn of humanity. In a sense magic is encoded in our DNA and is a part of our inherent sense of self, both in the personal and the divine (or holistic) sense. Each person acts according to personal programming. Magic is a process that attempts to move outside the box into the world of the boundless, where your reality can become what you want it to be.

For you to move outside the box, you need to get in touch with the person you truly are, meaning that you have to move beyond the preconditioned behaviors and pitfalls that everyone has to face in daily life. Rather than the good times, it is often the bad times that define who we are.

In magic, the best way to get through the bad times is to pivot. Pivoting in magic means that you are ready for anything that happens—and you have the ability to pivot in the situation in such a way as to turn it toward your advantage or, at least, keep it from being to your disadvantage.

When you become adept at pivoting, you progress further on your path to becoming a great witch or wizard. Magic is an art form that can often take years to shape completely into what you want it to be. It is an ongoing practice that continues and progresses throughout your life. You begin as a child of light, and in life you hope to realize this potential from the physical to the mental to the spiritual. Once you have woven magic into all the aspects of your life—body, mind, and spirit—then you begin to see positive change everywhere you look.

Whether Harry Potter or *The Lord of the Rings*, the battle being staged is always between light and dark. In life we often make choices that propel us in one direction or another. These are often choices between light and dark. In the end, we must all consciously aspire to bring the light into the world to combat the forces of darkness. Sometimes the divisions are not always clear, but your intuition will tell you the difference. Do not be taken in by the deception that sometimes professes to be light filled. Do not be taken in by the deception that often attempts to knock you off your true path.

Making magic ignites the witch or wizard within you. Just like Harry Potter, who waited until his eleventh birthday to realize his true destiny in the world of magic, you, too, can enter this realm to

realize all that you can be. It is a world in which anything and everything is possible. In the case of Frodo in *The Lord of the Rings*, he
came into his power and quest for light when he became entrusted
with the ring of power and had to face his own dark side as the
ringwraith.

Life is what you make it. Magic is a way of making you consciously
aware of what your choices are and how you can craft them into a
positive, healthy, joyful lifestyle. The more you deliberately influence
these choices, the more the magic begins to happen, and your life
will begin to resemble your dearest dream rather than your worst
nightmare. The most important thing is always to move into the light
rather than the dark, toward the positive rather than the negative,
toward love rather than hate, toward harmony rather than chaos.

The tone of your life is up to you. You can choose to toy with the
forces of darkness and struggle with life, or you can choose a melody
of light that leads you on your quest for magic and fulfillment of
your goals for life. The spells and rituals contained in this book are
presented as a means for helping you on your path of light.

Magic is something that comes from the divine union of the feminine (Goddess) and the masculine (God). This union is Oneness, a
place where all polarities come together. This is the place where all
life began and all life eventually cycles back to, in a huge spiral of
energy. This cycle has been going on since life began. The magic
seems to best happen when we directly tap into this source of life,
which we in a myriad of names term God and Goddess, Lord and
Lady, Mother and Father, and, in its holistic, united form, Oneness.

The influence of the divine in magic is significant. It powers your
spell casting. Many times when psychic healers touch the diseased
with their hands, the sick become healed with an invocation of the
divine spirits. Indeed the divine pushes the envelope every moment
and helps you move out of the box, out of your conditioned, ordi-
nary reality, and into a world of magic and mystery.

Magic is ultimately a process of expanding your mind, expanding
your boundaries, and becoming the magnificent person that you are

deep inside. It is all about freeing your mind, spirit, and imagination! The important thing is to make the choice for light. The spells and rituals in this book are all about helping you to make these correct choices, to help you on your quest to become a better witch or wizard. The important thing to remember through everything that happens on your life's adventure is that the magic is in you. You are the *magic!*

HOW TO USE THIS BOOK

You can use *The Witch and Wizard Spellbook* by itself or in conjunction with *The Witch and Wizard Training Guide*. The spells and rituals contained in this book are intended to help you become more familiar with the world of magic. Magic is said to be both an art and a craft. This is because of its creative aspect that in combination with magical techniques has been passed down for generations.

This book has three parts. Part I begins with instruction on collecting your magical tools, setting up your altar, and drawing a magic circle of light. Part I also gives a listing of the best times for doing different types of magic, including love spells and rituals for peace and prosperity. This section is divided into a planner for hourly, weekly, and monthly magical influences. Part I concludes with a sampling of magic spells that include a mind protection spell, a wand magic spell, and a shapeshifting and transformation spell.

Part II has spells and rituals that relate to the eight witch and wizard sabbats (Great Days). Beginning on Samhain, the traditional name for Halloween, and ending on the Autumnal Equinox, the sabbats progress on the path of the Sun through the cycle of the year.

Part III provides spells for the thirteen esbats or high moons from the Wolf Moon to the Oak Moon. The magical techniques presented include a dream incubation spell, a spell for getting in touch with your totem animal, and a spell for accessing the wisdom of your ancestors.

As you progress along your magical path, you will develop an understanding of what kind of magic works best for you. Through this you will learn both your strengths and your weaknesses. The idea in magic is to play to your strengths and work on your weaknesses until they, too, become strengths. Becoming a great witch or wizard means working to *realize* your full potential, gaining proficiency in all aspects of magic, and concentrating on the areas in which you excel. This is what I call "achieving magical balance."

Once you enter and begin working with the world of magic, you will begin to experience life on a different level. You will begin living the life that up to now has been only a dream. It is a flag that magic is indeed afoot when dreams begin becoming reality. The more time you spend in the world of magic, the more your dreams start coming true, until there is no division between reality and the dream. In magic they are one and the same.

The WITCH AND WIZARD SPELLBOOK

PART I

WITCH AND WIZARD MAGIC SPELLS

THE FIRST PART of *The Witch and Wizard Spellbook*, describes the magic toolbox, table, and circle. Your toolbox refers to the tools that you will need to do the spells. The table section gives instructions for setting up your magic altar, and the circle section explains how to draw a magic circle of light for doing magic and calling in the elemental powers.

Following the description of the toolbox, table, and circle, part I provides an hourly, weekly, and monthly planner that details the best times for casting specific types of magic spells. Part I finishes with a sampling of witch and wizard spells that you can use to do myriad things from bird augury and shapeshifting to improving your memory and summoning success.

Magic improves as you learn more techniques and continue to practice these techniques. What at first seems unfamiliar will, in time, seem easy, as if it was always a part of you. Like an adventure, the world of magic becomes more exciting and rewarding the further you proceed. Each spell moves you further along the magical path of the witch or wizard, following in the footsteps of such luminaries as Albus Dumbledore, Gandalf, and Glenda the Good Witch.

THE WITCH AND WIZARD TOOLBOX

In *Harry Potter and the Sorcerer's Stone*, the first thing Hagrid did was take Harry to Diagon Alley so that Harry could gather together his tools for his magical training. This points to the importance of magical tools when beginning your witch and wizard adventures. Broomsticks, wands, athames, crystals, essential oils, and herbs are just some of the tools that you will be using to create the magic spells presented in this book.

Your tools amplify the magical energy as well as provide you with a focal point for directing this energy toward your expectation and intention. As such, they open a door to a magical world that is waiting for you to enter and realize your potential as a witch or wizard.

You either make or buy your magical tools, depending on your situation and resources. Both this spellbook and the earlier one, *The Witch and Wizard Training Guide*, give detailed instructions for making a variety of tools, including a magic wand, a magic broom, and a magic cloak.

Whether or not you make them or buy them, your tools are an extension of yourself. This becomes increasingly so the more you use them. The following is a listing of the basic tools you will need to complete the magical spells and rituals in this book.

Athame: Symbolic of the creative fire, your athame is a double-edged knife or dagger that you purchase new. Its basic magical uses include cutting the magical circle, inscribing candles, and carving runes. For safety sake, the athame's edges are dulled. As with any knife, it should be kept in a safe place away from children.

Bell: Symbolic of the Goddess, rituals are usually begun and ended with the ringing of a bell. The other basic magical uses of the bell include cleansing a space, summoning divine energies, and serving as a fertility charm.

Book of Shadows: This personal magical journal provides you with a place to write down your rituals, potions, spells, thoughts, and dreams.

Bowl: Symbolic of the earth element, your bowl should be filled with either clean soil or salt. Magically, salt acts as a universal purifier and can be used to clean your personal space and all your stones.

Broom or **Besom:** Also known as a "Faery's Horse," the broom or besom dates back to ancient Egypt, where it was a wooden staff with an attached fan of feathers. Its magical uses include energetically cleaning your ritual circle, astral traveling, and handfastings. Please consult pages 19–20 of *The Witch and Wizard Training Guide* for detailed instructions for making your own magical broom.

Candles: Representing the fire element, candles act as a focal that makes it easier for you to enter the world of magic. Color, scent, and inscriptions are used in conjunction with candles to increase the power of your magic.

Cauldron: Symbolically housing the waters of life, magic cauldrons come in a variety of shapes and sizes, but all of them are three-legged pots with an opening smaller than the base. The magical uses for cauldrons include brewing potions, holding herbs, and scrying.

Chalice: Representing the element of water, the magical chalice or cup can be filled with either water or wine or fruit juice.

Cloak: Your cloak is what you wear when doing magic to give spells and rituals even more power. Akin to the skin of the Selkie, your magical cloak is one of your tools that helps you transcend the world of "Muggles" and move into the world of magic. Instructions for making your own magical cloak are given on page 23 of *The Witch and Wizard Training Guide*.

Clear Quartz Crystal: Pioneer inventor of liquid crystal display (LCD) technology, Marcel Vogel showed that clear quartz crystals vibrate at the same frequency as the human body. When you first use a crystal as a tool, it begins not only resonating with your energy but also amplifying that energy because that is the natural property of crystals. The spells and rituals in this book will introduce you to other crystals and gemstones that can also be used as magical tools.

Drum: As an audible focal, the drum is much like the candle, in that its presence and repetition creates an environment that is conducive to magic in its highest form. Drums, which can be anything that creates a percussive sound, can break up energy while moving you further into the magical world of witches and wizards.

Incense Censor with Incense: Symbolizing the air element, incense and incense burners are an essential part of your spells and rituals. Each piece of incense brings in an energy whose effects are particular to that specific flower, herb, and/or scent.

Staff: From *Indiana Jones* to *The Lord of the Rings*, the staff has been portrayed as an important magical tool that is used extensively by Gandalf the White in *The Lord of the Rings*. In the Harry Potter books, the staff represents the connection of the "Muggle" world and the world of magic.

Wand: Considered the inspiration of magic. The idea of the magical wand has evolved from a straightforward magical tool into an archetype. The idea that something can instantaneously transform matter from one shape to another is found throughout the world. The wand represents change in an essential way.

EMPOWERING YOUR MAGICAL TOOLS

The first thing you should do with your magical tools is to cleanse them of any unwanted energy. This is usually done by lighting a smudge stick until it smokes and then holding your tool in the smoke of the smudge stick until it is thoroughly immersed and feels clear of all energy. You can use the smoke of sandalwood incense in place of the smudge stick.

Another method for cleansing your magical tools is to wash them with dew before sunrise just before a full moon or sabbat (Great Day).

After cleansing your tools of any "old" energy, you then need to empower them with "new" energy so that they are ready for doing magic. Consecrating your tools involves blessing them with the elements. The salt or soil represents the element of earth, the smoke from the incense represents air, the candle flame represents fire, the chalice of water or wine represents water, and scented oil represents spirit. When empowering your magical tools, you need to apply the element actually to the tool. This means sprinkling salt on it, passing it through the incense smoke, moving it through the candle flame, sprinkling it with water or wine, and rubbing it with scented oil. After moving the tool through the elements, you should then hold it in your hands and present it to each of the four directions while moving in a clockwise circle. Stop in front of your altar and repeat the following verse aloud:

> *I charge this tool by the Ancient Ones,*
> *By the divine powers of the Goddess and God,*
> *By the powers of the sun, moon, planets, and stars*
> *By the powers of earth, air, fire, and water,*
> *May I attain all that I desire through this tool.*
> *Charge and bless this tool with your power Old Ones!*
> *Blessed be! As I will, so shall it be!*

Once you have cleaned and empowered your magical tools, then you are ready to start using them. When not in use, you can either leave them on your altar—if you have a permanent one set up—or put them away in a special place. I advise that you put your tools safely away to prevent other people from touching them. At least once a year, you should clean and reempower each tool.

COLOR CORRESPONDENCES

Color influences everything you see, and therefore it is a powerful tool in magic. Use the following table as a template for integrating color into your personal magical spells and rituals.

White   Universal candle color that can be used for all works. Inspiration, divine guidance, power, purity, love, motivation, peace, protection, Oneness

Gray   Mastery, balance, wisdom, merging, invention, discovery, protection

Black   Banishing negative energies, ending relationships, transforming negative energy to positive energy, representing the shadow self, dream magic

Blue   Tranquility, purification, healing, divination, travel, loyalty, psychic protection, perception, harmony, peace, moving energy, higher wisdom

Purple   Psychic awareness, ancestral lore, respect, sacredness, consecration, protection, dream magic, wisdom, spiritual healing, power, leadership

Pink   Friendship, romance, love, calming emotions, children, kinship, kindness, compassion

Rose   Ecstasy, divine love, enlightenment, romance

Red   Strength, survival, action, passion, lust, sexuality, vitality, virility, courage, blood, rebirth, focus, power, animation, intense desire

Orange   Business, joy, generosity, success, gladness, mirth, ease and comfort, prosperity, plenty, home, friendship, happiness, meditation, fair play, justice, productive action

Yellow   Attraction, persuasion, imagination, knowledge, learning, teaching, mental agility, understanding, cognition, truth, comprehension, communication, perception.

Green   Fertility, creativity, birth, healing, ambition, prosperity, abundance, money, regeneration, renewal, growth, nature, good luck

Brown   Grounding, stability, pets, animals, potential, nurturing, birth and rebirth, family, home, common sense

Gold   Wealth, increase, attraction, expanded awareness, creativity, strength, security, solar energy.

Silver   Peace, dream magic, lunar and stellar power, ancestral communication, divine insight, clairvoyance, astral travel, divination

THE WITCH AND WIZARD TABLE

Once you have gathered all your magical tools together, it is time to begin setting up your altar. As the sacred table of the Goddess, your altar is a connecting point to the divine and magical energies of Oneness as well a working surface to hold your tools, focals, and other items. Because of this, you will often find yourself standing before or continually going back to your altar while you practice your spells and rituals. Essentially, your altar is a platform reaching into the world of magic.

Your altar should be located on a sturdy surface, such as a table, countertop, mantel, tree stump, or large flat rock. Because you set up your altar in the north point of the circle, your altar should be an object already in the north quadrant or something, such as a table, that can be moved to the north point. Depending on your situation, you can either leave your altar set up at all times or set it up each time you do magic.

The reason the altar should be set up in the north is that north is the direction of divine knowledge and ancestral wisdom. Before placing your tools on the altar, begin by spreading an altar cloth out on the surface. The altar cloth serves both to protect the surface from things such as candle wax and to provide a magical focal during spells and rituals. Traditionally, altar cloths were red and made from natural fabrics, but in these ever-changing times, you can use whatever fabric or color works for you. If you like, you can decorate your altar cloth with magical symbols such as stars, moons, spirals, and runes.

The altar reflects the polarities of energy that relate to magic. The left side symbolizes the feminine polarity of the Goddess—an energy that is both creative and nurturing. The right side symbolizes the male polarity of the God—an energy that is strong and powerful. The center of the altar symbolizes the divine union of the Goddess and God. This union is known as Oneness, and represents the place where all things—no matter who, what, where, how, and why—become one. When energy becomes One is when real magic happens.

When placing your tools on your altar, consider the polarity of each tool. The bowl and chalice are feminine objects and should therefore be placed on the left-hand side, and the athame and incense burner reflect the male polarity and are traditionally placed on the right-hand side of the altar. The center is reserved for tools that reflect Oneness and spirit, such as your rings, essential oils, and clear quartz crystal.

While continuing your magical adventure, you will at times feel the urge to change your altar to reflect your current level of magic and your surrounding environment. Your altar reflects who you are and what is happening around you. Feel free to add a seasonal focal to your altar as a way to increase the power of your magic.

THE WITCH AND WIZARD CIRCLE

You can create magical enclosures in a variety of shapes. These include a circle, square, triangle, double triangle, sphere, pyramid, castle, V, and a star. Each shape gives a different nuance to your magic spell and ritual. You might use a square if you are doing magic that relates to career, a triangle if it relates to the spiritual, a sphere if it relates to the Earth, a pyramid if it relates to bringing energy into your life, a castle if it relates to the home, a V if you want to bring fire into your magic, and a star if you are working on a magic pentacle.

All these magic enclosure shapes are sacred geometry forms, as are mandalas, labyrinths, medicine wheels, and wheel of the year. Sacred geometry is the ancient sign language of divine light, nature, and creation. It is a cornerstone to understanding how the universe was formed as well as how to formulate and direct magical power. The most basic of geometric shapes contains within it a doorway that opens to other realms of consciousness. Thus, it behooves every aspiring and practicing witch and wizard to learn more about sacred geometry. As you focus, work, and move through the sacred shapes, your mind expands, and you begin to integrate these empowering, ancient patterns into your everyday life.

The circle is the shape most witches and wizards use when making magic and casting spells. The circle symbolizes the cycle of the seasons and eternal union of Goddess (divine feminine) and God (divine masculine) known as Oneness. For the purposes of this book, I will explain how to create a traditional circle. You will find examples of other powerful sacred enclosures interspersed throughout this book.

Usually, you will draw a circle before doing spellwork. The magical tools you will need to cast the circle are a compass, an athame, and a bowl of salt. If you do not have an athame, you can use either your wand or a clear quartz crystal instead. Begin the process by using the compass to find the north direction, and then, facing north, begin to spin slowly clockwise with your arms stretched outward. In your mind's eye, envision a clear blue light cleansing the area, while saying:

> *May all evil and foulness be gone from this place*
> *I ask this in the Lady's name.*
> *Be gone, now and forevermore!*

Starting at the north point again, take up your athame and draw a circle around the area that you are going to use for your magic. As you do this, imagine a blue light with white tips coming out from your athame and spreading around the perimeter of your magic circle of light.

Take a pinch of salt from the bowl and scatter it toward the north point while saying:

Ayea, Ayea, Kerridwen!
Ayea, Ayea, Kernunnos!
Ayea, Ayea, Ayea!

Depending on your personal preferences, you can invoke the Goddess and God of your choice. I use Kerridwen, the Celtic Mother Goddess, and Kernunnos, the Celtic Father God, because I feel the strongest rapport with these particular divine energies. After spreading the salt and cleansing the north point, move on and do the same thing to the east, south, and west points in individual order, while saying:

Ayea, Ayea, Kerridwen!
Ayea, Ayea, Kernunnos!
Ayea, Ayea, Ayea!

After completing these invocations, face the altar, and firmly say:

I consecrate this circle of power to the Ancient Ones
May they bless this circle with their presence.
Blessed be! Blessed be all who are gathered here.

Conclude the casting of your magic circle by knocking nine times in three series of three on the altar with the base of your athame or wand. You are now ready to call in the elemental powers.

CALLING IN THE ELEMENTAL POWERS

In each of the four directions of your circle is an elemental gate that leads to the Otherworld. Calling in the elemental powers sets a guardian at each of these gates to protect your circle while you are doing magic. These guardians remain in place until you release them and pull up your circle.

Begin by facing north and stretching both of your arms upward toward the sky. While merging with the earth element, say:

Guardians of the north march,
Generous powers of earth,

> *Protect the gate of the north ward,*
> *And guard this circle and all within.*
> *Come, I summon you!*

Next, turn and face the east point of your circle. Stretch your arms upward, merge with the air element, and say:

> *Guardians of the east march,*
> *Generous powers of air,*
> *Protect the gate of the east ward,*
> *And guard this circle and all within.*
> *Come, I summon you!*

Turn and face the south point. Stretch your arms upward, merge with the fire element, and say:

> *Guardians of the south march,*
> *Generous powers of fire,*
> *Protect the gate of the south ward,*
> *And guard this circle and all within.*
> *Come, I summon you!*

Face toward the west point, and stretch your arms upward. While merging with the elemental powers of water, say:

> *Guardians of the west march,*
> *Generous powers of water,*
> *Protect the gate of the west ward,*
> *And guard this circle and all within.*
> *Come, I summon you!*

Finish the process by standing in the middle of your magic circle. Face toward your altar, and say:

> *Guardian spirits of earth, air, fire, and water*
> *Grant me your power and protection tonight!*

The elemental powers now stand guard at the elemental gates of your magic circle.

CUTTING THE LITTLE GATE

I generally do not like to leave the circle once I have set it up for magic, but sometimes circumstances are such that you have to go out and come back into the circle. With this in mind, the "little gate" offers a way to physically move in and out of the circle without disrupting the magical energy.

Traditionally, the little gate is cut at the east point of the circle, but depending on where you have your circle set up, you may want to cut the gate at the door. Cut the gate with your athame or clear quartz by holding it in your dominant hand and by cutting a small energetic gate in the circle. Each time you want to leave or enter the circle, open the gate with a sweeping gesture of your power hand and move through the energetic perimeter of the circle.

Your circle is cast, and you are now ready to do that magic that you do so well. Once you are finished with your magic, it is important to bid farewell to the elemental powers, thank your energetic helpers, and pull up the circle.

BIDDING FAREWELL TO THE ELEMENTAL POWERS

I sometimes leave a circle up when I want to use it to keep generating more magical power and energy, and I know someone will not come in and physically disrupt the energy of the circle. For the sake of practicality, I usually pull up the circle when I am finished making magic. To pull up the circle, you first bid farewell to the elemental powers that you invoked when you initially set it up.

Begin at the north point, and say:

> *Generous powers of earth, depart in peace.*
> *Many thanks for your presence.*

Next, face toward the east point, and say:

> *Generous powers of air, depart in peace.*
> *Many thanks for your presence.*

Now, face south, and say:

> *Generous powers of fire, depart in peace.*
> *Many thanks for your presence.*

Last, turn west, and say:

> *Generous powers of water, depart in peace.*
> *Many thanks for your presence.*

PULLING UP THE MAGIC CIRCLE

Begin at the north point, but instead of clockwise, pull up the circle by using your athame or crystal and move around the circle counterclockwise, imagining the blue light with white tips moving back into your athame or crystal.

Finish closing your magical circle by knocking three times with the base of your athame or wand on the altar. Your circle is now pulled up, waiting for the next time you cast your magic spells. The next section on magical timing gives an overview of the best times for doing spell work.

WITCH AND WIZARD TIMING

When planting a vegetable garden, success depends a lot on knowing the optimal time to plant a particular crop. Magic is much the same way in that witch and wizard timing plays an important part in the process. Performing a spell or ritual on a Sabbat (Great Day) or Esbat (Full Moon) adds greatly to your magic just as planting corn seeds in the spring after the last frost adds to the level of your fall harvest. This timing in terms of the Great Days relates back to some of our most important days of celebration, including Yule (Christmas), Ostara (Easter), and Samhain (Halloween).

Magical timing stems from the influences that occur at any moment in the spectrum of time. These influences may include divine, planetary, numerological, and practical considerations.

The following section is an overview of the best times for doing magic. The time sequence is subdivided into hourly, weekly, and monthly planners. In addition, part II of this book deals with spells and rituals revolving around the Sabbats, and part III deals with spells and rituals revolving around the esbats.

THE WITCH AND WIZARD
HOURLY PLANNER

For the hourly planner I have listed two basic methods for determining the best magical timing for spell casting. The first method relies on numerological influences and the second relies on metaphysical influences.

Numbers correspond to the different hours. For hours above the number 9, add the numbers together: for example, the number 10 becomes 1 plus 0, which equals the number 1. Numbers 11 and 22 either can be taken as their total or can be broken down as 2 and 4. The choice is yours.

  1—Oneness, individuality, beginnings, initiation, and creation
  2—Partnership, balance or polarities, working with others
  3—Divinity, magical power, the Otherworld, communication
  4—Foundations, the four directions, construction, structure
  5—Magic, travel, change, power, adventure, and resourcefulness
  6—Home, family, love, beauty, the creative arts, and children
  7—Wisdom, the seven chakras, birth, spirituality, faith
  8—Reward, success, prosperity, the number of infinity, leadership
  9—Compassion, tolerance, completion, knowledge
  11—Intuition, spiritual healing, visions, and psychic abilities
  22—Mastery, mystery, rebirth, grand-scale networking

The eight times of the day are given along with how their metaphysical energies influence magical timing:

Dawn—The beginning of the day signals a time of renewal, rebirth, new ideas dawning, new beginnings, and consecration.

Morning—As the day's light grows stronger, so does your magic. An excellent time for setting patterns in play, for preparing potions, and for casting spells for attaining goals.

Noon—The magical energy of the Sun is greatest at high noon.

Afternoon—The heat of the afternoon sun makes the afternoon a good time for harvesting magical goals.

Dusk—Because it is the time when the portals to all worlds are thrown open and you can freely enter them, dusk is a very potent time for magic making.

Dark of Night—The time when the lunar and feminine energies are strongest.

Midnight—A good time to update your life patterns, practice dream magic, and let go of any negative energy you may be harboring.

The Hour Before Dawn—As with dusk, this is the time when the veil between the light and the dark is thinnest. This is the time when Otherworld beings, such as faeries, are most likely to come out.

THE WITCH AND WIZARD WEEKLY PLANNER

Each day of the week has influences that affect it magically. The basics of these influences are outlined in the following listing:

Monday: *Divine influence*—The Goddess; *Planetary influence*—The Moon; *Magical influences*—A good time for doing spells and rituals that relate to jobs, female fertility, psychic abilities, dreams, and beginning projects.

Tuesday: *Divine influence*—Norse God Tyr; *Planetary influence*—Mars; *Magical influences*—A good time for doing spells and rituals that relate to courage, personal power, passion, business, conquering enemies, and breaking negative spells.

Wednesday: *Divine influence*—Norse God Woden (Odin); *Planetary influence*—Mercury; *Magical influences*—A good time for doing spells and rituals having to do with divination, wisdom, learning, creativity, communication, and psychic awareness.

Thursday: *Divine influence*—Norse God Thor; *Planetary influence*—
Jupiter; *Magical influences*—A good time for doing spells and rituals
dealing with money, good luck, contracts, legal matters, expanding
business, political power, and male fertility.

Friday: *Divine influence*—Norse Goddess Freya; *Planetary influence*—
Venus; *Magical influences*—A good time for doing spells and rituals
that relate to happiness, musical skill, artistic ability, love, romance,
friendship, beauty, and sexuality.

Saturday: *Divine influence*—Roman God Saturn; *Planetary influence*—
Saturn; *Magical influences*—A good time for doing spells and rituals
dealing with property, inheritance, protection, agriculture, life patterns, structure, and resolution.

Sunday: *Divine influence*—The God; *Planetary influence*—the Sun;
Magical influences—A good time for doing spells and rituals relating
to healing, success, peace, harmony, and divine power.

THE WITCH AND WIZARD
MONTHLY PLANNER

The monthly planner uses the twelve astrological signs and their
influences on magical spells and rituals as the basis for the listing.

1. **Aries**, the Ram (March 20 to April 19) *Magical influences*—Aries
   is a fire sign, and this is a good time for building personal strength,
   adventuring, persisting, activating new ventures, stimulating
   moment, and meeting challenges.

2. **Taurus**, the Bull (April 19 to May 20) *Magical influences*—
   Taurus is an Earth sign, and this is a good time for fostering
   creativity, love, fertility, security, sensual desire, determination,
   generating abundance, artistic inspiration, and developing physical strength.

3. **Gemini**, the Twins (May 20 to June 21) *Magical influences*—
   Gemini is an air sign, and this is a good time for balancing polarities, communication, ideas, curiosity, compromise, and developing
   psychic abilities.

4. **Cancer**, the Crab (June 21 to July 22) *Magical influences*—Cancer is a water sign, and this is a good time for creating emotional balance, encouraging fertility, promoting mothering, protecting and blessing home and family, and exploring past lives.

5. **Leo**, the Lion (July 22 to August 22) *Magical influences*—Leo is a fire sign, and this is a good time for furthering your career, increasing productivity, expressing yourself, building magical power, fathering a child, improving self-esteem, exhibiting prowess, showing leadership, and demonstrating generosity.

6. **Virgo**, the Virgin (August 22 to September 22) *Magical influences*—Virgo is an Earth sign, and this is a good time for attending to details, organizing, structuring, improving employment, working with other people, and healing.

7. **Libra**, the Scales (September 22 to October 23) *Magical influences*—Libra is an air sign, and this is a good time for discovering or enhancing romance, love, and relationships; balancing energies; fostering creativity; and making new friends.

8. **Scorpio**, the Scorpion (October 23 to November 21/22) *Magical influences*—Scorpio is a water sign, and this is a good time for shapeshifting, creativity, passion, exploring mysteries, exploring the past and future, inheritance, and sex magic.

9. **Sagittarius**, the Archer (November 21/22 to December 21) *Magical influences*—Sagittarius is a fire sign, and this is a good time for changing bad luck to good and for traveling, expanding knowledge, changing perceptions, and being optimistic.

10. **Capricorn**, the Goat (December 21 to January 19) *Magical influences*—Capricorn is an Earth sign, and this is a good time for experiencing prosperity, advancing your career, being practical, showing discipline, giving order to your life, building ambition, developing patience, and improving your public image.

11. **Aquarius**, the Water Bearer (January 19 to February 18) *Magical influences*—Aquarius is an air sign, and this is a good time for delving into the unknown, practicing mysticism, inventing new concepts and things, using astrological knowledge, stimulating action, and promoting change.

12. **Pisces,** the Fish (February 18 to March 20) *Magical influences*— Pisces is a water sign, and this is a good time for connecting with the divine, delving into dream magic, enhancing intuition, using your imagination, communicating with ancestors, and increasing healing powers.

THE WITCH AND WIZARD MOON PHASE PLANNER

Each day the moon rises about fifty minutes later than the day before, leading to a cycle where the new moon always rises at sunrise and the full moon always rises at sunset. By knowing this, you can always tell where in the cycle of phases the moon is just by noting when it rises. When you watch the moon rising later and later in the evening, you know it is in its waning phase.

Each phase of the moon influences the power of your magic. The following listing gives what each phase is and explains how each affects your spells and rituals:

New Moon (night of the new moon) *Magical influences*—Good for beginnings, particularly new magical patterns.

Waxing Crescent Moon (first seven days after the new moon) *Magical influences*—Good for crafting magical patterns, making changes, and making new and helpful associations.

Waxing Moon (seven to ten days after the new moon) *Magical influences*—Good for increasing good luck, attracting prosperity, working on creative efforts, and moving forward overall.

Gibbous Moon (ten to thirteen days after the new moon) *Magical influences*—Good for completing magical goals, working on personal growth, attracting friends, and doing love and prosperity spells.

Full Moon (night of the full moon) *Magical influences*—Represents the time when the lunar energies are at their apex. It is an excellent time for doing spells and rituals. See part III for the magical influences for each of the thirteen full moons of the year.

Waning Gibbous Moon (the seven days that follow a full moon) *Magical influences*—Good for stressing the positive relationships in your life and ridding yourself of negative relationships, addictions, and habits.

Waning Crescent Moon (seven days after the full moon to the new moon) *Magical influences*—Good for building powers of protection and overcoming obstacles.

Dark or Black Moon (no visible moon) *Magical influences*—Good for casting protection and invisibility spells and rituals, as well as meditating, dissolving ties, and finishing magical patterns.

MAGIC-MAKING BASICS

The basics of creating magic are intention, expectation, desire, and merging. When you cast a spell, you have a specific intention and expectation. The stronger your desire to attain your magical goal, the better the results will be. Desire is also something you can build up when casting spells by using music, aromatherapy, crystals and gemstones, body movement, prayer, affirmation, invocation, and memories.

Basically, merging is the cornerstone of all magic, and it kick-starts all spell casting. When you merge with Oneness, with divinity, with nature, with all things, as deeply as you possibly can, that is when the magic happens. The merging process acts as a carrier wave for your powerful thought energy. Remember, you are the *magic!*

Natural merging occurs, for example, when you fall in love or experience the splendor of nature or when you get into the *zone* while playing sports or while listening to your favorite music. The easiest way to merge at will is to take several deep and complete breaths and then let your mind flow into all things. Rather than focusing on one thing, allow your mind to flow outward and touch all things. When I merge, it feels as if I am floating in a boundless field of white brilliant light in which I am everything and nothing and more all at the same time.

THE 13 MAGIC STEPS

For best results, follow the 13 Magic Steps as they are outlined. Unless otherwise noted in the spell, always cast a magic circle, call in the elemental powers, and then invite helpful energies such as faeries, power animals, and deities into the circle. When you have completed the spell, always thank helpful energies, bid farewell to the elements, and pull up the circle.

When using candles in spell casting, be sure to allow them to burn down safely. Oftentimes this requires you to snuff the candle out with a sea shell, candle snuffer, or some other fireproof tool and then relight the candle the next day. Never leave lit candles unattended!

1. Write the spell in your book of shadows or journal. Also, write down exactly what you want to attain by doing the spell.
2. Note the date, time, and day of the week that you cast the spell.
3. Note relevant astrological information such as the sun sign and moon phase.
4. Gather your tools and ingredients together, and set up your altar.
5. Draw a magic circle with your wand, athame, or dominant hand (V, square, sphere, pyramid, triangle, or star).
6. Invite helpful energies such as deities, faeries, and power animals, into the circle.
7. Cast the spell.
8. Write any comments, suggestions, or personal observations in your book of shadows.
9. Thank the helpful energies when you are finished spell casting.
10. Bid farewell to the elemental powers.
11. Pull up the circle.
12. Make certain the candles safely burn down, and clear your altar table.
13. Do something to clear your mind and bring you back to the present time and place. A few examples are take a bath, clap your hands, dance, sing, eat food, drink a refreshing beverage, play

catch with your dog, feed your cat, or go outdoors and look up at the sky.

WITCH AND WIZARD SPELLS

Each spell in this book is formulated as a complete work. When beginning your spell casting, I recommend following the instructions as presented. Once you become more adept at magic, go ahead and tailor the spells to fit your personal needs better, for example, by changing the invocations. Keep in mind, the more you enjoy your spell-casting adventures, the better your results will be. So have fun!

LOVE SPELLS

Friday nights when the moon is waxing or full are traditionally the best nights to cast love spells, unless otherwise noted. The witch and wizard sabbats are also powerful days to cast love spells.

SPECIAL ELFIN FRIEND SPELL

Soft music   Rosemary-scented oil
A piece of tumbled malachite

CASTING THE SPELL
The purpose of this spell is to connect with your special elfin friend so that he or she can help and advise you when you require it. Cast this spell at sunrise just before a full moon or on a sabbat. Turn on some soft music, and draw a magic circle. Draw another circle of light on top of the magic circle using bright green light. Anoint yourself with the rosemary-scented oil. Also known as elf leaf, rosemary encourages helpful elves and expands your awareness. Recline or sit comfortably, hold the piece of malachite in your left hand, and say:

> By the light, from north, east, south, and west,
> I call upon the helpful elfin powers of the forest.

Take several deep and complete breaths to relax and center your awareness. Listen to the rhythm of your breath. Now slow your breathing down by breathing in for three counts, holding your breath for three counts, and then exhaling completely. Feel your heart beating like a drum at the center of your being. In your mind's eye, imagine being in a magical forest, filled with elves and faeries and all other sorts of friendly spirits. As you enter the forest, you find a sweet spot, a place that feels very comfortable, to sit down on. It is early morning, just after dawn. The ground you sit on is still damp with the earth's sweat, and all you touch is moistened by the invisible morning dew. The melody of the dawn caresses your senses as you listen to the birdsong in the trees above you. As you sit quietly and wait, you feel as though you are glowing with inner radiance. You wait for your special elfin friend, a magical forest being. The colors of the new morning crystallize in the new sunlight, and you sit gazing through the brilliant light, feeling completely safe in the womb of the woods, as visions of your special elfin friend appear in the sunlight. You wait to become one with the forest, and your thoughts are suspended as the elfin essence of the forest calls you.

Levels of joy and hope course through you like water over your skin. Your elfin friend appears and looks at you. Time stops. You find kindness and love in the green forests of your elfin friend's eyes. Your friend speaks to you, and his or her voice sounds like a divine melody. He or she tells you his or her name. You hear harmony and hope in the soft tones of your friend's honeyed voice. As you reach out to your elfin friend, memories of lifetimes awaken. Spend a few minutes with your elfin friend, asking any questions you may have and listening for the answers. Oftentimes you may intuit, or sense, the answers. Now imagine your elfin friend merging with the sunlight. Know that you can communicate with your elfin friend anytime you want by holding the tumbled malachite in your left hand and saying:

> By the light, from north, east, south, and west,
> I call upon my special elfin friend named [say his or her name].

APOTHEOSIS LOVE SPELL

Passionate love music   Frankincense incense
Your magic wand   A white candle
A bowl of earth   A chalice of water

CASTING THE SPELL

The purpose of this spell is to elevate your love to a divinely romantic and passionate level. Turn on some passionate love music, a selection that propels you into a loving mood. Draw a magic circle, and call in the elemental powers. Use your magic wand to draw two circles of rose-colored light on top of the magic circle of white light. Light the candle and dedicate it to a favorite love god. Light the incense and dedicate it to a favorite love goddess, for example Venus or Aphrodite. Take the bowl of earth from the altar. Face north and scatter three small pinches of earth at the north point. Merge with the earth element, and say:

> *By the divine, loving power of earth*
> *Two as one, one as two*
> *You with me, me with you.*

Set the bowl on the altar, and pick up the incense censor. Carefully wave the incense back and forth at the east point. Merge with the air element, and say:

> *By the divine, loving power of air*
> *Two as one, one as two*
> *You with me, me with you.*

Set the incense censor on the altar, and carefully pick up the candleholder with the lit candle. Wave the candle back and forth at the south point three times. Merge with the fire element, and say:

> *By the divine, loving power of fire*
> *Two as one, one as two*
> *You with me, me with you.*

Set the candle on the altar. Pick up the chalice of water, dip your fingers into the water, and then scatter a few drops at the west point. Do this three times. Merge with the water element, and say:

> *By the divine, loving power of water*
> *Two as one, one as two*
> *You with me, me with you.*

Set the chalice on the altar. Stand at the center of the circle, and say:

> *By the divine, loving power*
> *Of earth, air, fire, and water*
> *Two as one, one as two*
> *You with me, me with you.*
> *One as two, two as one*
> *As I will, the spell is done!*

When you have finished, bid farewell to the elements and pull up the three circles of light. Return the soil and water to the earth.

RED ROSE QUICK SPELL

A red rose   A pillowcase

CASTING THE SPELL

The purpose of this spell is to strengthen your bond with your beloved. At midnight on a full moon, face east, hold the rose upward between your hands, and say:

> *Before the next rising sun*
> *[Insert your beloved's name] and my love will grow stronger*
> *And blossom like this beautiful rose*
> *As I will, so shall it be!*

Face west, and say:

> *Before the sun shall set*
> *[Insert your beloved's name] and my love will grow stronger*

And blossom like this beautiful flower
As I will, so shall it be!

Take each of the petals of the rose off, one by one, placing them in a pile. As you remove each petal say,

Our love grows stronger, so shall it be!

Tuck the rose petals in your pillowcase for three days to encourage your love to blossom and grow stronger.

Midnight Dancing Love Spell

Your beloved
Soft slow dancing music
A red pillar candle

A ballpoint pen or quill
Ylang-ylang–scented oil

Casting the Spell

The purpose of this spell is to create a magical night of romance with your beloved. Cast it on a Friday at midnight just before, or on, a full moon. Turn on some favorite slow dancing music. Open the circle and call in the elements. Use the pen or quill to inscribe the candle with your initials and your beloved's initials, surrounding them with a heart. Dress the candle with the scented oil, and wipe any remaining oil from your hands. Light the candle, dedicating it to love. Turn off the lights. Anoint each other with the scented oil. Take your beloved's hands in yours and say,

My heart is one with your heart,
My body is one with your body,
My soul is one with your soul.
Come dance with me, sweet love
Let the music carry us away!

Begin to slow dance together, very slowly and sensually, paying attention to every movement and feeling. Express your love and appreciation to your partner, and enjoy an extraordinary evening filled with

music, dancing, and love! At the end of the evening, bid farewell to
the elements and pull up the circle. For the next six nights, burn the
candle for at least an hour. On the last night, allow the candle to
burn down safely.

BLUE FLAME WISH SPELL

A purple candle   Lavender-scented oil
Your magic wand

CASTING THE SPELL

The purpose of this spell is to draw your love to you. Cast this spell
on Friday night on, or just before, a full moon. Draw a magic circle,
and then use your wand to weave a sphere of blue light all around
you. Do this by pointing your wand tip at the north point and spin-
ning slowly in a clockwise circle while imagining bright blue light
streaming out from your wand tip and flowing out all around you in
the shape of a large brilliant sphere. Call in the elemental powers.
Dress the candle with a thin film of lavender oil and anoint yourself
with a few drops of scented oil at your wrists, ankles, throat chakra,
heart chakra, and back and crown of your head. Wipe any remaining
oil from your hands, and light the candle. After you light the candle,
gaze into the flame, the bluest part of the candle flame and say:

> On this magical loving night
> In the candle's blue flaming light,
> I wish [name of person] were mine
> [Name of person] is truly divine.
> Blessed be! So mote it be!

Continue gazing at the flame and imagine your lover coming to you
in the near future. Do this for at least fifteen minutes as you merge
with the flame. When you have finished, bid farewell to the elemental
powers, and pull up the circle. Allow the candle to burn down safely.

Feather, Coin, and Flower Love Spell

1 sheet of purple construction
paper
A silver gel pen
Sandalwood incense

3 pinches of lavender flowers
A silver coin
A small white feather
A lavender candle

Casting the Spell

The purpose of this spell is to strengthen your love and bring more love, joy, and romance into your life. Draw a magic circle, and call in the elemental powers. Light the candle, and dedicate it to your favorite love goddess, for example, Venus. This invites the love goddess into your circle. Use the gel pen to write in large letters your beloved's name or the name of your would-be love on the sheet of purple paper. Write your name on top of your beloved's name. Fold the sheet of paper in half with the lettering inside. Tape the folded paper closed along two sides, leaving the third side open much like an envelope. Put the lavender flowers into the envelope pocket. Bathe the silver coin and feather in the incense smoke for a minute or two. Put the coin and feather into the envelope pocket as well. Tape the end shut. Use the gel pen to draw magical symbols such as stars, circles, moons, and runes on the outside of the charm. Hold the charm upward between your hands, and say:

> *I call upon the ancient, shining powers*
> *Unite our hearts with this coin, feather, and flowers.*
> *Fill this love charm with your light*
> *With harmony, beauty, and passion bright.*
> *May our love grow stronger in every way*
> *Bring us love, joy, and romance every day*
> *So be it! By the Lady, blessed be!*

When you have finished, bid farewell to the elements, thank the love goddess, and pull up the circle. Allow the candle to burn down safely.

Put the charm on your altar. Each day for twenty-one days, hold the charm in your hands and repeat the invocation to activate its powers.

SWEET LOVE GODDESS SPELL

A vial of vanilla-scented oil   A red candle
A tiny white stone

CASTING THE SPELL

The purpose of this spell is to put more sweet love in your life. For best results, cast it on a full moon. Draw a magic circle, and call in the elemental powers. Wash the small stone thoroughly. Inscribe the words *sweet love* on the candle body. Invite a favorite love Goddess into your circle by chanting her name nine times, in three series of three, for example, "Venus, Venus, Venus." Put the stone into the vial of oil. Hold the capped vial, and slowly roll it between your palms. As you do, continue to chant the name of the love Goddess, and imagine the divine love from the Goddess flowing into the scented oil. Do this until the vial becomes warm.

Next, dress the inscribed candle with a thin coat of oil, rubbing the oil first on the middle of the candle and moving outward toward both ends of the candle. Anoint your ankles, wrists, neck, and back of your head with a few drops of the vanilla oil. Wipe any remaining oil from your hands, light the candle, and dedicate it to your favorite love Goddess. Now gaze at the candlelight, or a reflection of the light, and focus all your attention on the one that you love, and say:

> *May we discover the true power of our sweet love*
> *May we discover the bliss and harmony of our sweet love*
> *By the powers of earth, air, fire, and sea, blessed be!*

Continue thinking about your beloved while the candle burns down. When you have finished, bid farewell to the elements and pull up the circle. Keep the oil on your altar, and anoint yourself with a few drops whenever you are with your beloved. Each time you anoint yourself say three times:

Blessed be our sweet love.

COLOR MY WORLD WITH LOVE SPELL

Hearts of bright colored paper
   (red, orange, yellow, green,
   blue, purple, and white)
A photo of your beloved or
   would-be beloved

A large white envelope
A red felt or gel pen
A green felt or gel pen

CASTING THE SPELL

The purpose of this spell is to imbue your relationship with your beloved with the vibrant colors of the rainbow. Cast this spell just after sunrise. The moon emits a light by which colors are not discernible, but as soon as the sun rises, all the colors can be seen. Put the hearts fashioned from the colored paper and the red and green pens in front of you where you can easily reach them. Take three deep, complete breaths. Focus on the photo of your beloved or would-be beloved. Now look at the red paper heart for a few moments.

Close your eyes, take a deep breath, and imagine breathing red loving light into the image of your beloved. Open your eyes and look at the orange paper heart. Close your eyes, take a deep breath, and imagine breathing orange loving light into your beloved's image. Open your eyes, and gaze at the yellow heart. Close your eyes and breathe yellow, golden loving light into the image of your beloved. Open your eyes, and look at the green heart. Close your eyes, and imagine breathing in loving green light into the image of your beloved. Open your eyes, and gaze at the blue heart. Close your eyes, and imagine breathing in blue loving light into your beloved's image.

Open your eyes, and look at the purple-colored heart. Close your eyes, and breathe in loving purple light into the image of your love. Open your eyes, and focus your attention on the white heart. Close your eyes, and breathe in white loving light into the image of your beloved for at least fifteen minutes. When you have finished, take a few deep, complete breaths, and open your eyes. Put the photo and hearts in the large envelope. Use the red and green pens to draw sacred symbols on the envelope such as hearts, moons, stars, runes, and crosses. Put the envelope under your bed for at least twenty-one days for best results.

THE EYES HAVE IT LOVE SPELL

Amber-scented oil   Love music

CASTING THE SPELL

The purpose of this spell is to connect with the divine essence of your partner by gazing into each other's eyes. When you look at a person, your gaze acts as a carrier wave, transmitting and directing your intention on that person. Light moves in through your eyes, and your mind flows out through your eyes. Your perception shapes your reality. With your love partner in hand, draw a magic circle of rose-colored light. Call in the elemental powers. Sit facing each other and anoint one another with the scented oil. Hold hands and gaze into each other's eyes for at least twenty minutes. When you have finished, bid farewell to the elemental powers and pull up the circle.

BIRD AUGURY LOVE SPELL

A feather that you find   Birdseed
A bird feeder

CASTING THE SPELL

The purpose of this spell is to divine your true love. Birds are messengers of the sun and heavens, expediters of the arrival of spring, and powerful protection against evil. Augury is receiving communication signs from birds. It is one of the oldest forms of divination. Sometimes you can be guided by the call, flight, and feather of a bird to your true love. Begin by finding a feather in nature. This feather is your divine sign from nature. Refer to the magical feather color meanings to understand the divine sign better. Fill the bird feeder with the birdseed. As you do, chant:

> *Seeds of nature*
> *Seeds of spring*
> *Divine my true love*
> *As the birds sing.*

As the birds eat the seed, your true love will fly into your life and grow stronger.

Magical feather color meanings are:

White	Birth, initiation, love, joy
Blue	A gift, love, happiness
Green	Adventure, dreams, abundance, growth
Rose	Romance, love, desire, divine union
Red	Courage, good fortune, love, passion
Purple	Journey or trip
Yellow	Friendship, companionship
Orange	Future happiness
Brown	Good health and happy home
Gray	Peace of mind, tranquility, harmony, wisdom
Blue and White	A new love
Brown and White	Good health and happiness
Gray and White	A new, happy event

MIGHTY DRAGON ATTRACTION SPELL

A handful of fresh or dried   A bowl
    sage herb

CASTING THE SPELL

The purpose of this spell is to draw your beloved to you. On a clear
night, on or just after a new moon, take the bowl filled with the sage
and go outdoors to a private place where you can perform this spell
without being disturbed. Look up at the night sky and find the
dragon among the stars, the circumpolar constellation Draco (Northern Hemisphere). It is located between Ursa Major (Big Dipper) and
Ursa Minor (Little Dipper). The body of Draco the Dragon looks as
if it were holding the Little Dipper. Cast a magic circle around you,
and call in the elemental powers. Call in the power of the dragon, the
power of the star constellation Draco by saying:

> *Mighty Draco, I invite you into this circle*
> *By the power of the winged dragon, so be it!*

Take the bowl of sage and sprinkle some of the herb at the north
point of the magic circle. Move clockwise around the inside of the
magic circle, and slowly sprinkle the sage in a spiral pattern. As you
do this, chant:

> *Mighty Draco guide my love to me.*

Stars generate and transmit energy in spiral form, so you are mirroring that pattern with the sage. Stand or sit in the center of the spiral
and take a few deep, complete breaths while gazing at Draco and the
stars surrounding it. Whisper to the stars:

> *Brilliant stars of light*
> *Blessed guardians of the night*
> *Please guide my love to me*
> *So be it, blessed be.*

Continue stargazing for several minutes, all the while focusing your attention on drawing your love to you. When you have finished, thank the Mighty Draco, bid farewell to the elements, and pull up your circle. Use your foot to blend the sage into the earth, leaving the area as natural as possible. As you blend the sage into the earth, whisper over and over:

Guide my love to me, blessed be.

HEALING AND BLESSING SPELLS

Always cast your healing and blessing spells when the moon is waxing. For the most powerful results, do healing spells on Sundays on, or just before, the full moon, unless otherwise noted. The witch and wizard sabbats are also prime times to cast healing and blessing spells.

ECO-NATURE HEALING SPELL

A living tree

CASTING THE SPELL

The purpose of this spell is to send healing energy to the Earth. From the ocean, the wind through the trees, and the songs of birds, you can hear the melodies of the seasons. These melodies are ever-changing, yet ever-remaining the same. But will the melody continue? Humankind is metaphorically slamming the CD into the concrete with greed and deceit. Our public and private forests are being butchered, our air polluted, our streams, rivers, and oceans poisoned—all for so-called profit. The only way we can overcome the impending destruction of nature and ourselves (as we are part of nature), is to make an effort and start working in harmony with nature.

It is time to learn from the natural wisdom of the plants, animals, fish, insects, earth, sky, and stars, all of which have inherent wisdom.

Cast this spell at dusk on a Sunday evening on, or just before, a full moon. Stand next to a favorite tree and place both your palms on the trunk of the tree. Take three deep, complete breaths and imagine any tension flowing out of your body with your exhalations. Merge with the tree, with nature, by becoming energetically one. Say:

Dear Mother Goddess and Father God, hear me now,
Please shine your divine light upon my prayer.
May the earth be healed and in harmony
By north, east, south, west, and center
By witch, wizard, fae, elf, dwarf, winged dragon, and dryad,
So be it! Blessed be!

Leave your palms on the tree for a few more minutes. Visualize the earth being healed and in harmony. Imagine all the positive magical energies and powers from all directions healing the earth, healing the minds of humankind so that we can learn to honor and love Mother Earth, rather than trying to destroy her.

ELEMENTAL MANTRA SPELL

A sheet of paper   A pen

CASTING THE SPELL
The purpose of this spell is to connect more closely with the elements in nature. Cast this spell at sunrise on a new moon. On the sheet of paper, write the following:

My flesh and bones are the earth
The earth is my flesh and bones
We are one.
My breath is the air
The air is my breath
We are one.

My eyes are the light
The light is my eyes
We are one.
The water is my emotions
My emotions are water
We are one.
I am all things and nothing and more
Nothing and all things and more are me
We are one. Blessed be!

Go outdoors at sunrise. Face the rising sun. Read the words on the sheet of paper aloud. As you read the words corresponding to the earth element, pick up some earth in your hands and feel it in your fingers. As you read the words regarding air, take a deep and complete breath of air into your lungs. As you read about light, face the morning sun and allow its warmth to caress your face. As you read about water, swallow deeply. Alchemically, the element earth relates to body salts, minerals, and bones. Earth associates with form and structure and corresponds to your nerves and brain. Air relates to the content of your mind, your lungs, and your body gases and to your ears and hearing. The fire element provides the heat and energy in your body, the light of your eyes and bioenergy, and corresponds to oxidation and consumption. The water element regulates your body's blood, oils, water, and their fluidity, as well as your responses to the moon and tidal flow. The more times you cast this spell, the closer will be your rapport with nature and the elements therein.

UNICORN LONGEVITY SPELL

Silver and gold gel pens
A black sheet of construction
  paper
A small pouch or bag
A glass or ceramic pot

A cup
1 cup unfiltered apple
  juice
3 teaspoons honey
A pinch of cinnamon

CASTING THE SPELL

The purpose of this spell is to encourage longevity by tapping into the magical power of the unicorn. Use the silver and gold pens to write the words "May the power of the unicorn shine upon me" on the sheet of black paper. Write these words three times. Fold the sheet of paper in half three times. Each time you fold the paper say:

> *Unicorn light, shine bright!*

Use the pens to draw stars and moons and other magical symbols on the outside of the folded paper. Put the apple juice, honey, and cinnamon in a ceramic or glass pot. Warm the potion very slowly. Stir the brew often. Each time you stir it, chant:

> *Potion of apple, spice, and honey*
> *Bring me good health and longevity!*

Pour the potion into a cup, and let it cool enough to drink. Hold the folded paper in your other hand and, as you slowly sip the potion, close your eyes and imagine a beautiful white unicorn with a golden horn standing in front of you. Imagine a warm radiant white light, a healing light, shining brightly all around the unicorn. As you gaze at the unicorn, the light surrounding it flows into you and fills you with its magical essence. You feel yourself being imbued with the magical light of the unicorn, a light of long life and eternal hope. Breathe in this sacred white light all the way into your being, into your body, mind, and spirit. Do this for several minutes, and when you feel the time is right, thank the unicorn spirit, bid farewell to the elemental powers, and pull up the circle. Put the folded paper in the small pouch or bag, and keep it somewhere safe and undisturbed.

SIRIUS STARWALKING SPELL

A clear quartz crystal

CASTING THE SPELL

The purpose of this spell is to experience starwalking. The best time to cast this spell is at night on a new moon, or right before the moon rises. Just prior to your performing the spell, I suggest that you listen to uplifting music such as Moby's "We Are All Made of Stars," Led Zeppelin's "Stairway to Heaven," or Dave Matthews's "Satellite." Cast your magic circle, and call in the elemental powers in a private spot outdoors where you can clearly see the stars. When starwalking, you shift your awareness and access the divine healing powers of the stars. By moving your awareness through the stargates (energetic portals used by the Lakota Sioux, Cherokee, Egyptians, and Mayans, among others), to a specific star, you can bring back that star energy to help heal yourself. Begin by asking the helpful healing energies of the celestial heavens to help you during the spell. Take a deep breath in and out. Put the stone in your power hand, and focus your awareness on it. Merge with the stone for a few moments. Focus your attention on the night sky, and find Sirius, the brightest star. Once you see it, move your awareness upward toward the star. Move higher and higher, ever higher into the night sky, focusing your complete attention on Sirius.

Imagine walking toward the star as it comes closer and closer. As you move higher and higher, you feel lighter and brighter. You see an energy gate before you, and you walk effortlessly through it. As you do, you experience a soft, popping sensation. That sensation is a gate that souls use to enter and exit the many dimensions of the continuum, including the earthly one. As you glide through the stargate, there is a being of pure white light waiting for you. This is your star guide, a magical being who will answer one pressing question. Ask this being your question now. Then, listen for the thought-form reply.

Your star guide beckons to you, and you move closer to the star. As you move closer and closer, you realize that the star is alive with energy. It is its own being, evolving and very much alive. Continue to focus on the star energy, and allow yourself to become one with the star. You and the star are both made of star stuff. By starwalking through the sky, you reconnect with your own stellar heritage and cosmic roots. Your stellar self becomes a source of energy, with the stars themselves. As you become one with the star, your intuition grows stronger, as do your healing abilities and creative powers. You find yourself walking through more stargates, following the memory of a star map that dwells within your very cellular structure.

Each time you enter another stargate, you feel a popping sensation, as if you were entering and exiting the many bubbles of existence. Continue experiencing this for several minutes. Now just enjoy your starwalking adventure for about 30 more minutes. When you begin to get tired or lose focus, it's time to come back to the present time and place. When you have finished your starwalking, come back to the present moment by slowly opening your eyes and sliding back completely into your physical body. Clap your hands three times. Thank your star guide, bid farewell to the elements, and pull up the circle. As you fall asleep at night for the next three nights, hold the crystal in your power hand [e.g., right if you are right-handed) and imagine yourself climbing into the heavens and tapping into the divine healing energy of the stars.

THINKING CAP WISDOM SPELL

A stool   A red hat

CASTING THE SPELL

The purpose of this spell is to increase your mental powers and answer a pressing question. On a full moon, sit on the stool facing east. Draw a magic circle around you, and call in the elemental powers. Think about a pressing question you have; keep the question simple. Ponder the question for a few minutes. Put the red hat on. Slip it snugly about your head, and say:

> *Hat of wisdom*
> *Hat of my red*
> *Find the hidden answer*
> *Find what is in my head.*

Take a couple of deep breaths in and out, and spend some time analyzing the question from all different angles—from inside and out, sideways, backward, and frontward, and from above and below. Ponder the question and look inside yourself. Allow the answer to well up within you. Once you have the answer to your question, write the question and answer down in your book of Shadows, or magic journal. Note the date, time, place, and all other significant factors. When you have completed the spell, bid farewell to the elements and pull up the circle.

Elf Attraction Spell

Your magic wand   A green candle
A silver bell

Casting the Spell
The purpose of this spell is to draw the magical powers of an elfin helper to your home. House elves are like the magical brownies from Celtic folklore. They do all kinds of tasks for people. House elves are small creatures, but they are very powerful. They can defend their human friends with their magic powers and disappear at will. Unlike forest or river elves, house elves are short, with large ears, long, thin noses, and huge eyes. The best time to cast this spell is at midnight on a new moon. Ring the bell once, and use your magic wand to draw a magic circle. Ring the bell twice, and draw another circle of light;

this time project green light on top of the first magic circle. Ring the bell three times, and draw a third circle; again project green light on top of the second circle. Call in the elemental powers. Light the candle, dedicating it to the helpful elves by saying:

> *I dedicate this candle to the helpful elves*
> *May its light guide my elfin helper to my home.*

Gaze into the candlelight, and ring the bell three times. Imagine your elfin helper coming into your home and filling your home with light and positive magic. Think about what changes you would like to make in your home and how you would like to go about it. Be creative and have fun—think of magical ways to make your home a happier, hopeful, and more joyful place to live. Continue doing this for at least 30 minutes. When the time has passed, thank the helpful elves, bid farewell to the elemental powers, and pull up the triple circle with your magic wand.

DIVINE QUINTESSENCE BLESSING SPELL

A bowl of salt	A chalice of water
A white candle	A white feather

CASTING THE SPELL

The purpose of this spell is to bless the earth and her children. Cast it on a full moon for best results. Gather all the items you will need and put them on the altar. Draw a magic circle around you, and call in the elemental powers. Light the candle and dedicate it to Mother Earth. Face north, and scatter a few bits of salt at the north point of your circle. Set the bowl of salt on your altar. Hold the feather in your power hand, and face east. Wave the feather, as if flying, at the east point three times. Set the feather on your altar. Carefully hold the candle between your hands. Wave it slowly back and forth, three times, at the south point. Carefully set the candle on the altar. Hold up the chalice of water, face west, and sprinkle several drops of water at the south point of your circle. Set the chalice down and face your altar. Merge with the candle, with Oneness, and then say this blessing:

By earth, air, fire, water, and spirit
Great Mother Earth, please hear my call
Please bless my family and myself with good health
Please bless all of your people with good health
May your fertile valleys, hills, and mountains sustain us
May your divine light burn away the darkness
May your divine waters wash away our pain
May your gentle breezes blow away our sadness
Mother Earth, in your divine quintessence
Please bless us with your love and compassion
By earth, air, fire, water, and spirit
So be it! Blessed be!

Gaze at the candle for several minutes, sending the feelings behind the blessing into the world, to the people you love, and outward into the entire planet. When you are done, thank Mother Earth, bid farewell to the elemental powers, and pull up the circle. Allow the candle to burn down safely. Throw the salt away, and return the water to the earth.

DRAUGHT OF HARMONY AND PEACE SPELL

¼ cup papaya nectar
¼ cup apricot juice
¼ cup mango juice

¼ cup white grape juice
A pinch of fresh mint
A large glass

CASTING THE SPELL

The purpose of this spell is to bring more harmony and peace into your life and into the world. Cast it at sunrise on a new moon or on a witch and wizard Sabbat. Slowly stir the four juices together in the large glass. Add the pinch of mint. As you stir, say:

By the powers of earth, air, fire, and water
By the divine powers of the Lord and Lady
By the sacred, shining powers of the One
Please empower this potion.
May harmony and peace abound on Earth
May love and joy brighten our spirits
In waking and in dream
In all times and all places
As above, so below
So be it! Blessed be!

As you slowly sip the potion, imagine harmony and peace flowing into your life and into the world around you. Imagine love and joy brightening your spirit, and say a simple prayer that the world will be blessed with harmony and peace, now and forevermore. As you go about your day, keep harmony, peace, love, and joy in your heart and make an effort to uplift those around you with a smile, a kind word, and a hug.

BETTER MEMORIES SPELL

A blue candle   Rosemary-scented oil
A cup of mint tea, sweetened   A 13-inch piece of string
   with honey to taste

CASTING THE SPELL
The purpose of this spell is to bring better memories to mind and rid yourself of outworn, negative memories. Cast this spell on a new moon at midnight. Dress the candle with a thin film of scented oil. Anoint yourself with the oil. Wipe any remaining oil from your hands. Light the candle, dedicating it to a favorite healing Goddess or God or to the healing spirits of nature. Prepare a cup of mint tea. Before sipping the tea, focus your attention on it, and imagine filling

the tea potion with magical energy. Stir the tea several times, and chant over and over,

With this tea, better memories come to mind.
Blessed be! Blessed be! Blessed be!

As you drink the tea, imagine your memories becoming happier and more positive. Rub a few drops of scented oil on the string. Hold an end of the string in each of your hands, and slowly begin knotting it. As you tie each knot say:

Middle of middle, beginning of beginning, end of end
As I knot this string together, my memories I do mend.

Continue until the entire string is knotted together. Carefully drip candle wax over the knotted string, keeping the flame away from the string. Do this over a fireproof plate or an altar tile, for example, and avoid burning yourself or dripping hot wax on your household furnishings. When you are finished, let the string cool. Place the knotted, waxed string on your altar for at least twenty-one days to encourage better, more positive memories in this lifetime—and in other lifetimes as well.

WAND MAGIC HEALING SPELL

A small oak branch
(approximately the length
from your elbow to the end
of your outstretched fingers)

Green yarn
Chamomile tea
Lavender-scented oil
A recent photo of yourself

CASTING THE SPELL
The purpose of this spell is to create a healing wand. Cast a magic circle, and call in the elemental powers. Put the photo on your altar table for now. Just stick out your wand hand, your power hand, and

take hold of the wand. Shake it above your head three times. Wash
the oak branch with chamomile tea, and say:

> *By the powers of the sacred waters*
> *By the powers of the sacred tree*
> *Bless this healing wand*
> *With your divine energies!*

Allow the branch to dry, and then apply twenty-two drops of the
lavender oil on the wood. As you apply the oil, say:

> *By the powers of the sacred oil*
> *By the powers of the sacred tree*
> *Bless this healing wand*
> *With your divine energies!*

Wind the yarn carefully and firmly around the wand branch. Start at
the base, secure the yarn, and wind it up to the tip of the branch.
Secure the yarn end at the tip as well. Hold the wand between your
hands, face your altar, and say three times:

> *Blessed be this oak healing wand!*

Spread a thin coat of lavender oil on your photo. Hold the wand in
your power hand, and focus your mind on your image in the photo.
Point your wand tip toward the photo, and move it in small clockwise circles. As you do this, imagine the divine healing powers of
the oak wand flowing into your hands and out the wand tip into
your image in the photo. Say this healing prayer as you point to your
image:

> *By the powers of the healing wand*
> *By earth, air, light, and sea*
> *May the divine healing light of nature*
> *Restore and renew me.*
> *May the divine healing light of spirit*
> *Restore and renew me.*

May the divine healing light of love
Restore and renew me.
By the divine powers of north, east, south, and west
May I be divinely healed and blessed!

When you have finished, thank the healing spirits, bid farewell to the elemental powers, and pull up the circle. Keep your oak healing wand on your altar, and use it whenever you have the need.

MIND PROTECTION SPELL

A mirror   A red candle
Amber-scented oil   A pen or quill
A strand of your hair

CASTING THE SPELL

The purpose of this spell is to create a protective shield around you, using the powers of your ancestors. This spell will work whether or not you know who your ancestors are. Draw a magic enclosure, but instead of a circle of light, draw a star of light. The best way to do this is to draw two interlocking triangles that create what is called "Solomon's Shield." Also, draw a magic circle of white light around the two triangles. Inscribe the red candle with the words *mind shield*, then inscribe your initials on top of the words. Dress the candle with a thin coat of amber oil, and anoint your wrists, your ankles, your throat, and your crown and back of your head with a few drops of the oil. Wipe the oil from your hands, and light the candle.

Put the mirror next to the candle so that you can see its reflection in it and also your own reflection. Gaze at your reflection for a few minutes. Burn the strand of your hair in the flame of the candle to call your ancestors. Do this carefully to avoid burning your fingers. Ask your ancestors to impart their powers unto you, and ask them to shield you from unwanted energies by saying:

I call upon the helpful powers of my ancestors
Please protect and shield me from harm.
By the ancient ancestral power, blessed be!

Commune with your ancestors for at least fifteen minutes before bidding farewell to the elements and closing the circle. Allow the candle to burn down safely.

PROSPERITY SPELLS

The best days to cast spells for prosperity are Thursdays and Sundays on, or just before, a full moon, unless otherwise noted. The witch and wizard sabbats are also ideal times to weave prosperity and abundance into your life.

SUMMONING SUCCESS SPELL

Soft meditative music
9 white stones from nature
A large bowl of water

3 green or 3 gold floating
candles or both

CASTING THE SPELL
The purpose of this spell is to summon success and prosperity into your life. Cast this spell on, or just before, a full moon or on a witch and wizard sabbat. Turn on some soft meditative music. Draw a magic circle, and call in the elemental powers. Put the stones in the bowl. Fill the bowl with water. Float the candles on the water. Light the candles. As you light each candle, say:

Water and flame combine
Goddess and God divine
Divine cauldron of insight
Bowl of bright candlelight
I summon my success, my prosperity
By the Lady and Lord, blessed be!

Carefully stir the water with your power hand fingers, and watch the candles slowly float in the water. Imagine your success in the near future. Imagine your life being filled with prosperity and positive abundance. Imagine sharing your good fortune with others and attaining even more success and joy. Do this all the while the candles burn. When you are finished, bid farewell to the elemental powers and pull up the circle. Return the stones and water to Mother Earth.

OPEN OPPORTUNITY SPELL

A green candle   Cinnamon oil
A pen or quill

CASTING THE SPELL
The purpose of this spell is to create a door of opportunity for you. Cast this spell on a witch and wizard high (full) moon or sabbat. Draw a magic circle, and call in the elemental powers. Use the pen to write the letter *N* for north on the candle body, and draw a simple door around the inscribed letter, and say:

> *Powers of north, element of earth*
> *Open the door of opportunity.*

Spin the candle clockwise in your hands, and write the letter *E* for east. Draw a doorway around the inscribed letter, and say:

> *Powers of the east, element of air*
> *Open the door of opportunity for me.*

Spin the candle again, and write the letter *S* for south. Draw a doorway around the inscribed letter, and say:

> *Powers of the south, element of fire*
> *Open the door of opportunity for me.*

Spin the candle and write the letter *W*, for west on the candle body. Draw a doorway around the inscribed letter, and say:

Powers of the west, element of water
Open the door of opportunity for me.

On the candle bottom, inscribe the letter *C* for center. Inscribe a simple doorway around the letter *C*.

Powers of divine quintessence
Open the door of opportunity for me.

Dress the candle with a thin film of the cinnamon oil. You can make your own cinnamon oil by putting a pinch of dried cinnamon spice into a teaspoon of olive oil and mixing it well. Wash any remaining oil from your hands. (Cinnamon can be highly irritating if it comes in contact with your mucous membranes, so do not touch your eyes or other parts of your body with your fingers when covered with cinnamon oil.) Light the candle. Gaze at the candlelight for a while, and then close your eyes. Take a few deep breaths. As you do this, imagine an open doorway in your mind's eye. This is the doorway of opportunity. Shape the doorway in any way that you like to fit your needs and preferences. In your mind's eye, see yourself walking through the open doorway. As you imagine yourself walking over the threshold and through the doorway, visualize the opportunities you would like to have in the near future. Continue this visualization for at least fifteen minutes. Once you have accomplished this, bid farewell to the elemental powers and pull up the circle. Allow the candle to burn down safely.

SILENCE IS BLISS PROSPERITY SPELL

Pine-scented oil

CASTING THE SPELL

The purpose of this spell is to bring more prosperity into your life. Cast this spell after dark on a new moon. Make sure you work in a quiet place where you will not be disturbed. Anoint yourself with the pine-scented oil. Sit or stand comfortably and visualize a castle of white light in your mind's eye. Shape the castle with your imagination. Imagine entering the castle and standing inside its protective walls. Say the following invocation once you see yourself inside the castle walls:

> On this night and all nights
> In this world and all worlds
> At this time and all times
> I stand in the castle of light
> I stand in the silence of the night
> I stand at the divine crossroads
> I stand beneath the new moon
> I stand beneath the stars so bright.
> Radiant spirits, please hear my call
> I ask that my prosperity grow
> I ask that my joy grow
> In the moon's silent light
> As I will, so shall it be!

Imagine your prosperity and joy growing as the moon waxes and grows. Imagine being showered with abundance and joy. Continue this visualization for at least fifteen minutes. When you have finished, imagine stepping out of the castle of light and into the present time and place. Clap your hands three times. This will bring you back to the present time and place.

SALT, SULFUR, AND MERCURY QUICK SPELL

A sheet of paper	A match
A pen	A thermometer with mercury
A pinch of salt	A rubber band

CASTING THE SPELL

The purpose of this spell is to draw prosperity to you by utilizing alchemical basics. Cast this spell on a full moon. Draw a magic circle, and call in the elemental powers. On the sheet of paper, draw an equilateral (equal-sided) triangle of white light. Write the word *Mercury* above the top point of the triangle. Write the word *Sulfur* next to the right point of the triangle, and write the word *Salt* next to the left point. These three substances form everything that lies in the four elements. In these three substances exist the forces and faculties of all perishable things. Put the actual salt, the match (unlit), and the thermometer on top of the triangle. Fold the paper in half, and then roll it up (salt, match, and thermometer included) into a scroll. Secure the rolled scroll with the rubber band. Hold the scroll in your power hand and say three times:

> *By the trinity of salt, sulfur, and mercury*
> *Please bring me prosperity, blessed be!*

When you are finished, bid farewell to the elemental powers, and pull up the double triangle and circle of light. Put the scroll on your altar for at least twenty-eight days (one moon cycle) to draw prosperity into your life.

ANIMAL ABUNDANCE DREAM SPELL

Sandalwood-scented oil   Pictures of your power
                                              animals

CASTING THE SPELL

The purpose of this spell is to identify a power animal to dream with you and help you manifest abundance. On a partly cloudy day, anoint yourself with the sandalwood oil and go outdoors and gaze at the clouds. Look for the shapes of animals in the clouds such as winged dragons, birds, wolves, cats, rabbits, and elephants. Each animal has its unique magical energy. Once you identify an animal, write it down in your Book of Shadows. Continue your search for at least thirty minutes. Find or purchase pictures of a couple of the animals that you saw in the clouds. Study them before you go to sleep. Anoint yourself with the sandalwood-scented oil, and as you drift off to sleep, repeat silently to yourself,

> *Animals of power dream with me*
> *I will remember my dreams when I wake up.*

Repeat this for eight nights in a row. Write down the details you recall about your dreams when you wake up. Use this information and the helpful energies of your animals of power to draw more abundance into your daily life.

CELTIC BARD ENRICHMENT SPELL

Soft Celtic music   A pen or quill
A blue pillar candle   Dill or almond bread

CASTING THE SPELL

The purpose of this spell is to enhance your creative abilities in the arts. Cast this spell on, or just before, a full moon or on a witch and wizards sabbat such as Beltane or Yule. Turn on the music, draw a magic circle, and call in the elementals. Inscribe the words *Copper/ Venus* and *Tin/Jupiter* and *Lead/Saturn* on the candle body. Then, add the words *Iron/Mars* and *Quicksilver/Mercury* on the candle. Light the candle, and say:

> *Copper, tin, lead, iron, and mercury*
> *May the divine ancestral energies*
> *Of the Bard empower my creativity*
> *Forever and a day, blessed be!*

Merge with the candlelight, and take a few deep breaths. Move your awareness into the music. Imagine that you are the Bard of creativity. You are the melody and the rhythm. You become all sound and absolute silence. Each vibration of your being is infinite, and you are the continual, ever-beginning, never-ending cycle. You constantly change and forever remain the same. You are eternal imagination and the vibrant energy of all nature. You are the light and the darkness. Your name is whispered by the winds, and your face is found in every raindrop. You are the door, yet there is no door, only oneness. You flow with the music and allow it to act as a catalyst for your creative abilities. Imagine your creativity growing stronger and stronger. Visualize expressing your creative abilities and enjoying the experience. Continue this visualization for several minutes. When you feel it is time to bring it to a close, do so. Then eat the bread slowly. Dill and almond both encourage happiness and good fortune. As you eat the bread, continue thinking about your creative abilities expanding and expressing your talents in positive ways. When you have finished, thank the Bard, bid farewell to the elemental powers, and pull up the circle. Snuff out the candle. Allow the candle to burn for at least an hour, and then relight it and snuff it out every day for at least eight days. Every time you relight the candle, repeat:

> *Copper, tin, lead, iron, and mercury*
> *May the divine ancestral energies*
> *Of the Bard empower my creativity*
> *Forever and a day, blessed be!*

On the eighth day, allow the candle to burn down safely.

DRAGON FIRE TREASURE SPELL

A Celtic weave pin, brooch, or pendant

A bunch of fresh basil

Cedar-and-sage smudge

CASTING THE SPELL

The purpose of this spell is to empower you with dragon fire energy. Smudge the piece of jewelry for a few minutes to clear it of any unwanted energies. Draw a magic circle, and scatter pieces of the basil around the perimeter of the circle. Keep a bit of the basil, and softly rub it over the piece of jewelry nine times. As you rub the basil over the jewelry piece, repeat over and over:

Winged fire dragons of prosperity
Impart your ancient treasure unto me.

Hold the pin, brooch, or pendant in your power hand, and say three times:

Empower this pin [brooch or pendant] with dragon fire.

Actually imagine dragon fire pouring into the object; then, use your breath to move the intense dragon energy into the item by breathing in deeply, holding your breath for a few seconds while you focus on imparting dragon fire power into the object, and then sharply exhaling through your nose, not your mouth. Repeat this nine times. Your pulsed breath and focused intention are the carrier waves that move the energy into the piece of jewelry, consecrating it and making it sacred. Imagine wonderful riches and marvelous treasures coming your way for several minutes. When you have finished, thank the winged dragons, bid farewell to the elements, and pull up the circle. Every time you wear that piece of jewelry, activate its dragon fire powers by saying:

Winged fire dragons of prosperity
Impart your ancient treasure unto me.

SHIFTING SPELLS

(SHAPESHIFTING, POWERSHIFTING, TIMESHIFTING)

SHAPESHIFTING AND TRANSFORMATION SPELL

A quartz crystal
Your favorite incense
A candle holder in the shape
   of an animal such as an owl,
   wolf, elephant, or butterfly

A green candle
A chalice of water

CASTING THE SPELL

The purpose of this spell is to experience shapeshifting energetically in order to increase your magical knowledge. Cast it on a full moon or sabbat. You may not have the ability to turn into a tabby cat or white stag at will, but you can energetically experience shapeshifting, which often expands your mind and your perceptions of reality. Draw a magic circle, and call in the elemental powers. Light the candle, dedicating it to the nature spirits. Hold the quartz crystal in your power hand and focus your awareness on it. Merge with the stone, and say:

Transform and shift, inform and uplift.

Imagine stepping into the crystal. Shapeshift into the stone for a few moments, become one with it. Set the crystal on your altar, and light the incense. Watch the incense smoke waft upward. Merge with the air element, and say:

Transform and shift, inform and uplift.

Imagine you are the smoke flowing upward, higher and higher in the air. Shapeshift into the incense smoke for a few moments, and allow the air to uplift you. Shift your focus on the candlelight. Watch the flame as it moves, bobs, weaves, and flickers. Merge with the fire element, and say:

Transform and shift, inform and uplift.

Shapeshift into, and become, the candle flame for a few moments, allowing the power of fire to fill your body, mind, and spirit. Focus your awareness on the chalice of water. Hold it in your hands, and merge with the water element. Say:

Transform and shift, inform and uplift.

Slowly drink the water. Shapeshift and become one with the water. Feel it become one with your physical body. When you have finished, bid farewell to the elements and pull up the circle.

POWER ANIMAL SPELL

A piece of malachite   A silver candle
A bowl of tree leaves or pine
   or cedar needles

CASTING THE SPELL

The purpose of this spell is to contact your power animal helper. Cast this spell on a full moon. Draw a magic circle and use the leaves or needles to outline the circle. Call in the element powers. Light the candle, and say:

I dedicate this candle to the animals of the Mother Earth.

Hold the piece of malachite in your receiving hand, and say:

Form reveals essence
Body, soul, and mind
Like with like
Kind with kind
Blessed animal kin
Come into my circle
Feather, fur, and fin
Bless me with your presence.

Still holding the malachite in your receiving hand, sit or recline comfortably. Take a few deep breaths to relax and center yourself. Then close your eyes and visualize a magical forest in your mind's eye. In the forest, there is a tree covered with white flowers. Alongside to the tree is a clear-running creek with green ferns surrounding it. You can smell the scent of the water and the flowers. You breathe in deeply, feeling more relaxed and peaceful than before. Imagine sitting by the side of the creek and looking at the flowering tree.

As you look at the beautiful tree, you see a soft shimmering light coming from behind it. The shimmering light grows brighter and transforms into a beautiful animal. Use your inner eyes to see your power animal. Take a few moments, and look at the animal's beauty and sense its natural strength. Without fear, imagine touching your power animal, making contact. As you do, all the natural wisdom of the animal immediately passes into you. Ask the animal its name. If you have any trouble discovering your power animal's name, repeat your question and wait for a response. Repeat your power animal's name over and over again to yourself. Ask your power animal one question. Listen carefully for its answer. The answer may be nonverbal, more a thought form.

As you remain in contact with the animal in your visualization, imagine that its strength and power are merging with you and empowering you. Imagine becoming one with your power animal. Continue this visualization for at least fifteen minutes. When you have finished, thank your power animal for its help. Clap your hands three times. Now bid farewell to the elemental powers, and pull up the circle. In your Book of Shadows, write down your power animal's name, and record your question and the answer you received.

HARBINGER OF CHANGE SPELL

Your magic wand   Star stickers
A sheet of white paper   A small box
A blue felt pen

CASTING THE SPELL

The purpose of this spell is to make positive changes in your relationships at home and at work. Draw a star of white light instead of a magic circle. Do this with your wand, start with the topmost point of the star or pentacle and move down, then left, right, down, and up, in that order. Call in the elemental powers. Write the headings *Relationship*, *Home*, and *Work*, on the sheet of white paper. Write the one, most important thing you would like to change under each heading. Make sure it is a positive and helpful change. Slowly read aloud what you have written under each of the headings. Affix the star stickers to the list in a decorative way. Fold the paper nine times, and sit down in front of the altar. Hold the folded paper in your power hand, and squeeze it. Close your eyes, take a deep breath, and imagine that you have already made the changes that you wrote on the paper in your hand. Continue this visualization for at least five minutes.

Put the folded paper in the box. Take the box outside and look up at the bright sky for a few minutes. Focus on making the changes you desire. Hold the box between your hands, and repeat three times:

> Powerful stars of radiant light
> Help me make these changes tonight
> I bind the stellar power within this box.
> This spell is cast, and will hold fast!

Go back indoors, thank the star spirits, bid farewell to the elements, and pull up the star of white light. Put the box somewhere where you will see it every day to remind you to take the steps needed to make the desired changes.

TURNING TIME SPELL

A watch

A clock with a chime (or a recording of a chiming clock, see instructions)

Cedar-and-copal smudge

CASTING THE SPELL

The purpose of this spell is to stretch time psychically as a way to access specific information and wisdom. Cast this spell at the closest hour to sunset on a full moon, because you will be using the chiming of the clock to time the spell. The clock type determines its use. For example, use a clock that has been passed down to you or an antique clock to access ancestral wisdom. Use an animal-shaped clock to access that particular animal's wisdom, for example, a *Lion King* clock to bring out the lion in you, or a cuckoo clock to access your playful inner child.

If you prefer, you can record the sound of a chiming clock to use for this spell. A few minutes before the clock chimes, put the watch on and draw a magic circle. Call in the elementals. Light the candle, dedicating it to your favorite Goddess and God, to Oneness, or to the nature spirits such as those of your power animals, of the faeries, or of the elves. Use the candle to light the smudge. Purify your magical space with the smudge smoke. Extinguish the smudge completely when you have finished smudging. Just as the clock chime starts, slowly turn the watch hands forward. Three complete turns should do it. As you turn the hands forward, say:

> At the sound of the chime
> I travel through time.
> The veil lifts
> Time shifts
> Thrice turns the hour
> Bringing magical power.
> A moment becomes an eternity
> Wisdom whispers clearly to me.
> As I will, so mote it be!

Turn the face of your watch so that its face is illuminated in the candlelight. Gaze at the watch, and imagine turning an hour into three hours, giving you three hours of time, for example, to learn about your ancestors or to get in touch with your wild or playful nature. Sit back and enjoy the next hour, until the next hourly chime. Become one with the knowledge you seek as you stretch time. When the clock chimes on the hour, turn the hands of your watch back so that it reads the correct time, and say three times:

> At the sound of the chime
> I return to the present time.

When you have finished speaking, thank the divine powers, bid farewell to the elements, and pull up the circle. You can repeat this spell as often as you like.

LUMINOUS LIGHT SPELL

A large mirror   3 white candles
A hand mirror   3 fresh bay leaves
Sandalwood-scented oil

CASTING THE SPELL

The purpose of this spell is to commune with the divine energies of
the Goddess or God. The most powerful days or nights to cast this
spell are on high moons and the sabbats as the divine energies are
then at their highest peak. Even so, you can cast this spell anytime
you like. The more you do it, the better your rapport with the Goddess and God. Stand so that you can clearly see your reflection in the
large mirror. Draw a triple circle of white light around you, and call
in the elemental powers. Dress the candles with a thin film of scented
oil, and anoint yourself at the wrists, ankles, throat, and crown of
your head. Wipe the oil from your hands. Put the candles where their
flames can be seen in the large mirror. Light the candles, one at a
time. With each candle you light, say:

The Goddess and God walk with me, blessed be!

Take a few moments to study your reflection in the mirror. Nature as
the divine sculptor gives all living things essence and form. Nature
molds the form to fit the soul. In this way, the shape of your face and
your body reflect your heart and soul. As you study yourself in the
mirror, reflect on your positive qualities, your shining attributes. As
you look at your reflection in the mirror, say:

The Goddess and God walk before me, blessed be!

Energetically, the divine Goddess and God walk with you—before
and behind, beside on both sides, above and below you. Turn your
back on the large mirror. Tear the bay leaves open, and inhale the
heady fragrance that spills from them. Breathe in the bay scent a few
times. Hold the hand mirror so that you can see the reflection of

your back in the large mirror, and study your reflection. As you look at the reflection of your back in the hand mirror, say:

The Goddess and God walk behind me, blessed be!

Turn slightly so that you can see the reflection of your side in the large mirror as you hold the hand mirror, and say:

The Goddess and God walk beside me, blessed be!

Turn again so that you can see the reflection of your other side in the large mirror. Repeat:

The Goddess and God walk beside me, blessed be!

Turn again so that you can see your face in the large mirror, and in the hand mirror, and say:

The Goddess and God walk with me, blessed be!
Before and behind, beside, above and below
May the luminous light of the divine Mother and Father
Shine brightly upon me, now and forevermore
The Goddess and God walk with me, blessed be!

Gaze at your reflection and the reflection of the candlelight for a few more minutes and begin to see the divine qualities, the luminous light, that you possess. You may see the aura of light around you in the mirror. This is the luminous light that we all are born with. This is the luminous light that you may see around animals, trees, and flowers. Continue doing this for at least fifteen minutes. When you are done, thank the Goddess and God, bid farewell to the elements, and pull up the circle. Return the bay leaves to the earth.

TRADING PLACES SPELL

A white candle   Uplifting music
A picture or video of an ideal
  place

CASTING THE SPELL

The purpose of this spell is to expand your magical awareness. Cast it anytime, day or night, during the waxing moon. Use a picture or video of a place where you would ideally like to be. Put the picture where you can easily see it, or turn on the video (sound completely muted). Study the picture or video. Turn your mind to the image(s). Imagine stepping into the picture or video for a few minutes and being there. Trade places; move your awareness from here to there! Take a deep breath in and out, and in your mind's eye, imagine your-self there in the picture, experiencing the ideal place and fully enjoy-ing the adventure of trading places. Continue to experience this exchange for at least fifteen minutes. Take a few deep breaths, and clap your hands together three times when you have returned. Repeat this spell whenever you want to trade places and adventure to that magical place.

TWINKLING WATER SPRITE SPELL

A small cake   A bouquet of flowers

CASTING THE SPELL

The purpose of the spell is to draw the divine insights of the water sprites and helpful faeries to you. Cast this at sunrise the morning just before a full moon day or on a witch and wizard sabbat. Sit next to a body of water, for example, a stream, creek, river, natural pool, pond, forebay, reservoir, lake, or ocean. Draw a magic circle around the area where you are sitting. Use half of the flowers to outline the magic circle. Call in the elemental powers. Invite the water sprites and other helpful faeries into your circle by saying:

> *Helpful and friendly water fae*
> *Bless me with your presence today.*

Divide the cake in half. Offer half to the water fae by crumbling it finely and putting it in the water. As you do, say:

> *Friendly water fae from east, south, west, and north*
> *Twinkle bright and bless me, water sprites*
> *O gentle water spirits, come forth*
> *Please bring me magical insights.*

Put the other half of the flowers in the water, one by one. As you do, chant:

> *Twinkle bright, water sprites*
> *Please bring me magical insights.*

Sit quietly for at least thirty minutes and commune with the water spirits all around you. Ask them questions to which you seek answers. When you have finished, thank the water sprites and faeries, and pull up your circle. Scatter the flowers used to outline your magic circle on the water. As you do, say:

> *Thank you, friendly water fae*
> *Thank you for your blessings today.*

SECRET KEEPER SPELL

| A dark-colored cloak | Uplifting music |
| or blanket | |

CASTING THE SPELL
The purpose of this spell is to bring a secret wish to light. Cast this spell on a new moon. Turn on the music and put on your cloak.

Magical power rides under the cloak of the four primary concepts of love, wisdom, self-honesty, and self-responsibility. You can make a cloak by cutting out a large square or rectangular piece of fabric. Hem it all the way around. Drape the cloak and then pin it at the shoulders with a large brooch. Or you can create a poncholike cloak by cutting out a large circle of fabric and then cutting a neck hole in it. Cut the neck hole off-center to give the cloak a defined front and back. In a pinch, you can use a blanket draped around you.

Once you have put on your cloak, imagine entering the castle of white light. See and sense yourself inside the safe castle walls, surrounded by a cocoon of white light. Take a few deep breaths to center your awareness. Then think of one wish, some deep desire you have kept secret all these years. Make sure the secret desire passes the love, wisdom, self-honesty, and self-responsibility test. In other words, make sure it is a secret wish that will prove to be a win–win situation for all those involved. Spend at least fifteen minutes thinking about ways in which you might express your secret wish and attain it. Go over the steps that you need to take to manifest it. Think of one thing, one action step, that you can do to move closer to actualizing your secret wish. In the next week, take that action step! When you have finished, leave the castle, and move your awareness to the present time and place.

PART II

THE EIGHT WITCH AND WIZARD SABBATS

THE WHEEL OF THE YEAR, also called the "Path of the Sun," turns forward so that every forty-five days, a witch and wizard sabbat is celebrated. The four spokes of the wheel are the solstice and equinox points, which are the minor or lesser sabbats, with another four spokes halfway between each of the first four, which are the major sabbats. These are the quarter and cross-quarter days. The dates given for each sabbat are the days most witches and wizards celebrate them.

These eight sabbats are powerful times for casting magic spells. They are astrological power days when the energy for magic making is at its highest peak according to universal, alchemical patterns. The Old Style way of figuring the sabbats is according to the sun. Both ways of determining the sabbats are valid. Try them both and see which one works best for you. It also gives you more flexibility for spell casting as the sabbat energy is high for about a week. The Old Style sabbat chart is as follows:

Winter Solstice: sun 00.00 degrees Capricorn
Imbolc: sun at 15.00 degrees Aquarius
Spring Equinox: sun at 00.00 degrees Aries
Beltane: sun at 15.00 degrees Taurus
Summer Solstice: sun at 00.00 degrees Cancer
Lughnassad: sun at 15.00 degrees Leo
Autumnal Equinox: sun at 00.00 degrees Libra
Samhain: sun at 15.00 degrees Scorpio

The witch and wizard spells presented are tailor-made to tap into the natural powers of these days of high magic. Also provided are suggestions for decorating your magic altar. Remember, stay focused, be creative, listen to your heart, stretch your imagination, merge deeply, and have fun casting these magic spells!

SAMHAIN SPELL: OCTOBER 31

Halloween, All Hallows' Eve, The Great Sabbat

Magic altar decorations: A dark-colored altar cloth, 13 golden-orange leaves from a tree, pumpkins, gourds, witch and wizard figurines, faery lights, crystals and gemstones, runes, oghams, I Ching, tarot cards, and photographs of your ancestors.

Samhain, also called "Halloween," is fast becoming the second most popular holiday in North America, right behind Christmas. People carve pumpkins and give out candy and treats. Others dress up in costumes and go from house to house trick or treating. It is a terrific night to party!

The Irish word *Samhain* means "summer's end," foretold by the beginning of November, when the mysterious Pleiades stars rise. This time of year is associated with the eagle and Scorpio. At Samhain, the veil between this world and the Otherworld is most easily penetrated. It is also one of the foremost times for divination.

A carved pumpkin with a candle inside	Sage-and-cedar smudge stick
3 white candles	3 fresh bay leaves
A thumb-sized or larger crystal point	An apple

CASTING THE SPELL

The purpose of this spell is to find an answer for one personal question regarding the upcoming year. Cast it at midnight on the eve of Samhain. Before you begin, think of a personal question about the upcoming year that you would like answered. Write it down in your Book of Shadows, and note the date and time. Light the candle in the pumpkin. As you do, say:

Divine light, please guide me tonight.

Light the other three candles from the pumpkin candle. As you light each candle, say:

Divine light, please guide me tonight.

Light the smudge from the pumpkin candle flame. Bathe the crystal point in the smudge for a couple of minutes to clear it of any unwanted energies. Once the stone is cleared, completely extinguish the smudge stick. Put the crystal in front of the pumpkin and candles so that it is illuminated in their light. Take a few minutes to center your mind. Breathe deeply and let go of any residual stress you may be feeling with your exhale. Tear the bay leaves, and breathe in their fragrance for a couple of minutes. The Oracle at Delphi used the scent of bay to encourage travel into an altered state of consciousness. Take the crystal from the altar, and hold it between your hands. Imagine your energy moving into the stone so that you become one with it. Once the crystal warms in the heat of your hands, it is acti-vated for scrying or reading. Speak aloud three times the question you have written in your Book of Shadows. Focus your awareness on the question for a couple of minutes. Hold the crystal upward so that the candlelight illuminates its facets. Gaze into the stone. Study the patterns of light and shadow within the crystal. Turn the stone slightly in your hand to see more patterns within it. Merge with the patterns of light in the stone. Continue scrying the stone in this way for at least thirty minutes. During the same time ponder your ques-tion about the future year. As your mind flows with the crystal light, you may see images in the lattice of the stone, see images in your mind, or sense the answer to your question as a nonspoken word. Divination information comes to you in many magical ways, so above all, trust your intuition.

When you have finished scrying, write the answer you received in your Book of Shadows. Also make a note of any images or other information you may have received. Repeat this spell a maximum of three times if you desire more information. When you have finished, light the smudge from the pumpkin candle flame, and smudge the crystal thoroughly. Eat your apple. Extinguish the smudge. Bid farewell to the elemental powers, and pull up the circle. Allow the candles to burn down safely. Return the bay leaves and pumpkin to the earth in the morning. As you do, say:

Blessed be the light!

WINTER SOLSTICE SPELL: DECEMBER 20–22

Yule

Magic altar decorations: A red altar cloth, holly, ivy, mistletoe, red poin-settias, stars made of twigs, home-crafted ornaments, fir and pine boughs, living trees, and pinecones.

Yule signals the return of the light of the sun. Yule traditions include a lighted evergreen tree and the Yule Log. Hanging mistletoe and decorating your home with pine and fir boughs, pinecones, and holly branches reaffirm the theme of the rebirth of the sun. Gifts are also often exchanged as symbols of love and rebirth.

Another Yule custom is lighting the Yule Candle, usually a large ornamental blue, green, or red candle, which represents the blessings of the sun. Keeping a piece of wax from the candle brings good fortune and good health to you and your family during the whole of the new year.

Your athame
A large Yule Candle (blue,
   green, or red pillar)
A pen or quill

A small stone or metal pyramid
Sandalwood-scented oil
Mint tea with honey and
   lemon

CASTING THE SPELL

The purpose of this spell is to draw good fortune and good health to you and your family using the powers of the Yule Candle and the Witches' Pyramid. Cast this spell at sunset on the eve of Yule. Make a cup of mint tea and sweeten it with the honey and a little lemon. Slowly sip the tea as you sit or stand in front of your altar. Before you take the first sip, say:

> *May the divine powers*
> *Of good fortune and good health*
> *Be with me now. Blessed be!*

As you sip your tea, use the pen or quill to inscribe these words on your Yule Candle: *To Know, To Will, To Dare, To Keep Silent.* Dress the candle with a thin film of sandalwood oil. Anoint yourself with the oil. Draw a magic circle. Then draw a Witches' Pyramid inside the magic circle. The Witches' Pyramid is also called the Hermetic Quaternary because it presents the four principles of magic crafting: to know, to will, to dare, and to keep silent. As an ancient enigma from the earth's mysterious past, the pyramid is a powerful, timeless symbol. Draw an energetic pyramid of white light with your athame, cutting the base or foundation first. As you do this, say:

> *With the powers of the element of earth*
> *I am the foundation of the pyramid*
> *I know, I think, I learn, I question.*

Cut the right wall of the pyramid next. As you do, say:

> *With the powers of the element of air*
> *I am the right, the might*
> *I will, I intend, I create, I exemplify.*

Cut the left wall of the pyramid, and say:

> *With the powers of the element of fire*
> *I am the left, the flame*
> *I dare, I merge, I use my power wisely.*

Cut another circle of white light on top of the original circle you drew. As you do, say:

> *With the powers of the element of water*
> *I am that which surrounds all things*
> *I keep silent, I wait patiently, I attain success.*

Anoint the pyramid figurine with the oil. Put the figurine on the altar where you can easily see it. Wipe any remaining oil from your hands, and light the Yule Candle, and say:

> *I know, I will, I dare, I keep silent*
> *I am the pentacle and the shield*
> *I am the athame and the sword*
> *I am the wand and the spear.*
> *I am the chalice and the grail*
> *I am the pyramid of the light*

By center, north, east, south, and west
With good fortune and good health
May the new year be magically blessed!

Merge with the candle for several minutes. Imagine the new year exactly as you would like it to be. Imagine bridging time and space and moving your mind into the new year. See, hear, touch, taste, and smell the new year. Become one with your thought patterns about the new year and connect with them. Think locally and globally. Your thoughts are carrier waves for manifesting your intention into reality. Focus on the pyramid figurine, and merge with the powers of the Witches' Pyramid, with the elemental quintessence, with the four principles of I know, I will, I dare, and I keep silent. Continue for several minutes, and once you feel that you have finished, use your athame to pull up the pyramid and the circles of light in the order you laid them down. Allow the candle to burn at least three hours on the first night. Also, leave your Yule tree lights on the whole night for good luck. Relight the candle each day and allow it to burn for at least an hour. Each time you light the candle, repeat:

By center, north, east, south, and west
May the new year be magically blessed!

Repeat these actions each day until New Year's Day. On that day, allow the candle to burn down safely, except for one piece. Put that Yule Candle piece just inside your front door to bring you and your family good fortune and good health in the coming year. Keep the pyramid figurine on your altar to draw good fortune and good health to you and your family.

IMBOLC SPELL: FEBRUARY 1 OR 2

Candlemas, Oimelc, Bridget's Fire, Feast of Torches, Feast of Pan

Magic altar decorations: A gold or yellow altar cloth, bay leaves and sprigs, flowers, crystals and gemstones, and goddess and god figurines.

Imbolc, means "in the belly of Mother Earth." It is associated with the spirit and the time of Aquarius, when light and dark are equal. A time of weather prediction, the traditional rhyme goes, "If Candlemas be bright and clear, there'll be two winters this year." In fact, the cross-quarter days can be used to predict inverse weather patterns, while the quarter days can be used to predict direct weather patterns. It is also the time of the first lambing, when flower bulbs poke their heads out of the earth.

Imbolc is also a fire festival, dedicated to the Celtic Goddess Bridget, the Bride, symbolizing the first signs of life being rekindled. Bridget is a triple goddess who represents the earth and the soil's fertility. She is a strong, intense feminine force as well as a powerful ally for witches and wizards. She is the goddess of hearth and home, writers, poets, artisans, smiths, healers, and craftspersons. Her name means "bright one."

Lavender essential oil
Neroli-scented oil
Vanilla oil
A golden-colored bell
3 gold or 3 yellow candles
A large bowl of clean soil
Fresh golden or yellow flowers
Joyous music

CASTING THE SPELL

The purpose of this spell is to celebrate three magical blessings. Cast this spell after dark on the eve before Imbolc. Begin by filling your bathtub with warm, but not hot, water. (If you prefer, you can shower instead, adding the three oils to your washcloth or loofah sponge.) Into your bathwater put three drops each of lavender essential oil, vanilla-scented oil, and sandalwood-scented oil. As you add the drops, say:

One, two, three, blessed be!

Bathe (or shower) for about ten minutes. As you do, repeat silently to yourself:

I am empowered by my blessings.

Carefully step out of the tub, dry off with a soft towel, anoint your wrists with a drop or two of the oils, and then get dressed. Draw a magic circle, and call in the elementals. Ring the bell three times. Put the flowers in a vase on your magic altar. Dedicate them to Bridget by saying:

I dedicate these flowers to the bride of the sun.

Inscribe the candles with three things you are thankful for. With each candle that you inscribe, say:

Goddess of divine light
Thank you for this blessing
By the grace of the Lady, blessed be!

Draw arrows, pointing toward your writing, on the candle bodies as well. Dress the candles with the scented oils, one type per candle. Put the candles in the large bowl of soil, and position them in a reversed triangular configuration on your altar. Anoint yourself with the oils as well. Wipe any remaining oil from your hands. Light the candle in the middle. Ring the bell three times, and say three times:

I am thrice blessed by the Goddess
Blessed be the divine trinity!

Light the candle on the left from the middle candle flame. Ring the bell three times, and repeat three times:

> *I am thrice blessed by the Goddess*
> *Blessed be the divine trinity!*

Light the candle on the right from the left candle flame. Ring the
bell three times, and repeat three times:

> *I am thrice blessed by the Goddess*
> *Blessed be the divine trinity!*

Turn on some joyous music. Dance a circle dance, sing, and shout.
Music is myth, mirth, metaphysics, and magic. It is a magic beyond all
magics. When you are done, ring the bell nine times. Thank the
Goddess Bridget, bid farewell to the elemental powers, and pull up
the circle. Allow the candles to burn down safely. In the morning, get
dressed and go outdoors just after sunrise when the birds are singing.
Face the sun, and say,

> *Bridget, Bridget, Bridget, brightest flame*
> *Bridget, Bridget, Bridget, sacred name*
> *One becomes two becomes three*
> *Thank you, dear Lady, for my blessings!*

Return the soil and flowers to the earth, and say:

> *Blessed be the bride of the sun!*

SPRING EQUINOX SPELL: MARCH 20–22

Ostara, Lady's Day, Hertha's Day, Vernal Equinox

Magic altar decorations: A green altar cloth, living flowers, seed packets,
seed pods, eggs, egg-shaped stones, twigs, rabbit and chick figurines, your magic besom (broom), and 12 new tree leaves.

Ostara was an ancient Teutonic Goddess of Spring and an even
more ancient Aryan Goddess of the dawn. With a rabbit as her

animal familiar, Ostara, whose name in Old English translates to Oestre, was the pagan Goddess from whose name Easter is derived.

A planting and fertility festival, Ostara heralds the reemergence of life from its winter slumber. It is the custom to decorate eggs with the symbols of the goddess. Eggs are then hidden, rolled down hillsides, tossed and caught, and eaten on this day. Slavic peoples have been practicing this art since 5,000 B.C.E. Eggs are related to the powers of the sun and the eternal cycle of creation and life. Their magical powers encourage good fortune, good health, wealth, joy, and protection from harm. Seeds are also planted as a tribute to the goddess as the cosmic egg within Mother Earth is reborn.

A green candle
A pen or quill
Your magic wand

3 hard-boiled decorated eggs
Your magic besom (broom)

CASTING THE SPELL

The purpose of this spell is to draw good fortune, good health, wealth, and joy to you and to protect you from harm. Cast this spell after dark on the eve before Ostara. Put everything on your magic altar. Face your altar with the broom in your hands. Take a deep breath, and imagine sweeping away all outdated, outworn things in your life. Do some personal spring-cleaning, and make room for good fortune and good health in your life as you sweep away all the negative energies. Actually, use the besom to gently sweep your magical space, moving clockwise and sweeping from the middle outward. With each sweep you make, say:

With this broom,
I sweep all negative energies from this room.

Draw a sphere of white light in place of a magic circle. Do this by cutting the energy sphere with your wand, and imagine actually walking into the white sphere of light. See and sense it surrounding

you completely—above and below, in front and behind, and on both
sides. It is as if an egg of white light envelops you. Call in the elementals. Use the pen or quill to draw a circle with a cross inside it on
the candle body. Hold your wand in your power hand, and point it
at the candle. Circle the candle three times, clockwise with your
wand. Light the candle and say:

> One, two, three, blessed be
> My good fortune and wealth are flowing
> My good health and joy are growing
> By the sacred powers of sun and spring,
> Protect me from all harm! Blessed be!

Circle the basket of eggs three times, clockwise, with your magic
wand. Repeat:

> One, two, three, blessed be
> My good fortune and wealth are flowing
> My good health and joy are growing
> By the sacred powers of sun and spring,
> Protect me from all harm! Blessed be!

Use your broom to sweep good fortune, wealth, joy, and good health
into the room and into your home and life. Take a few deep breaths
so that you can better focus your awareness on your magical work.
Sweep clockwise, but sweep from the outside inward toward the
center of the circle this time. Turn your mind toward sweeping all
the good things into your life. With each sweep you make, say:

> With this broom
> I sweep positive energies into this room.

When you have finished, bid farewell to the elements and pull up the
sphere of white light. Put the eggs in the refrigerator and eat them,
saving the shells. Return the eggshells to the earth. As you do, say:

> Blessed be the sacred powers of spring!

Beltane Spell: May 1

May Day

Magic altar decorations: A red and green altar cloth, herbs (such as lavender and rosemary sprigs), tree boughs, flowers (such as irises, snapdragons, daisies, and roses), maypoles, heart shapes, photos of your beloved, wedding or handfasting rings, and other tokens of love.

Coming down from the sky to the shores of Ireland from the east in a cloud of mist, the Tuatha de Danann arrived in Ireland on Beltane morning. They were the ancient inhabitants of Ireland and the divine race of people in Old Irish mythology, often called the "Shining Ones," who later became the Goddesses and Gods of Celtic mythology. Beltane translates as "the fires of Bel," as Beli (Belenus) is the Celtic God of the rising sun, and whose name means "bright."

Beltane is the time of the year when spring is in full bloom. Associated with the bull and Taurus, it is the witch and wizard sabbat of love, fertility, and renewal of nature, second only in importance to Samhain. It signals the return of romance, love, passion, desire, and hope. May flowers are worn by the May Queen and King, and the maypole (obviously phallic) is joyously danced around. Also, Beltane bonfires are lit from a spark emitted by friction or flint. Once lit, everyone dances clockwise around the Celtic Holy Round, the sacred bonfire.

Rosemary essential oil
Cedarwood essential oil
A fine-mist spray bottle
A green candle
A yellow candle
Rose-scented oil
A cauldron
Flowers
A stick (about 24 inches long)
Three pieces of white ribbon (each about 18 inches long)

Casting the Spell

The purpose of this spell is to empower your love and create a stronger primary relationship. Cast this spell at moonrise on the eve before Beltane. Fill your cauldron with flowers, and put it on the altar. Draw a magic circle, and call in the elemental powers. Fill the fine-mist spray bottle with the water, and then add ten drops of the rosemary oil and five drops of the cedarwood oil. Cap the bottle. Shake it, and say three times:

Magic mist, empower me!

Now spray the mist over your head several times with your eyes closed. Breathe in the aroma. Dress both candles with a few drops of rose oil. Slowly and sensuously rub the scented oil into the wax. As you do so, imagine the love you would like to bring into your life tonight on Beltane. Picture your beloved's image or your would-be love's image, clearly in your mind. Imagine exactly the kind of relationship you desire, with the qualities of love, caring, and pleasure, that you cherish. Wipe any remaining oil from your hands. Put the green candle in a candleholder and light it. Call the energy of the nature faeries into your circle by saying the following:

I dedicate this candle
To the helpful spirits of the nature fae,
May my love grow stronger each and every day.

Place the yellow candle in a candleholder, and light it. Call the energy of the sun into your circle by saying the following:

I dedicate this candle to the divine light of the Sun,
So my love will seed, grow strong, and blossom.

Tie an end of each piece of ribbon to one end of the stick so that all three pieces are on one end of the stick. Hold the stick in your hand by the end opposite the ribbon. Move to the north point of the circle, and shake the stick up and down three times while saying:

Element of Earth,
Please bring your strength of love into my life
As I will, so shall it be!

Move to the east point of the circle and shake the stick up and down three times while saying:

> *Element of Air,*
> *Please bring your breath of love into my life*
> *As I will, so shall it be!*

Move to the south point of the circle, and shake the stick up and down three times while saying:

> *Element of Fire,*
> *Please bring your passion of love into my life*
> *As I will, so shall it be!*

Move to the west point of the circle, and shake the stick up and down three times while saying:

> *Element of Water,*
> *Please bring your flow of love into my life*
> *As I will, so shall it be!*

Now step into the middle of the circle and, beginning at the north point, slowly spin around clockwise while saying:

> *From the sacred fire of the God,*
> *Love keeps shinning through,*
> *From the sacred well of the Goddess,*
> *Life begins anew.*

Stop at the north point, and say:

> *Please divine Goddess and God,*
> *Grant me my true Beltane desire,*
> *May my love be forever fueled,*
> *By the warmth of Bel's divine fire.*
> *As I will, so shall it be! Blessed be!*

Spin slowly in two more clockwise circles, all the while repeating:

> *Please grant me my true Beltane desire.*

Face the altar and gaze at the candle or at its reflection while imagining divine love flowing into your life every day. When you have finished, bid farewell to the elemental powers and pull up the circle. Respectfully thank the spirits of the faeries and flower devas as well as the divine energy of the Goddess and God. If possible, spend the night outdoors with your beloved, and greet the sun together. At sunrise on Beltane morning, walk barefoot on the green grass for a while until your feet are wet with the morning dew. As you walk, chant softly:

> *Blessed be the power of love*
> *Beating the bounds, as below so above*
> *From north, east, south, and west,*
> *By the morning sun, I am blessed!*

When the flowers are spent, return them to the earth. As you do so, say:

> *Love keeps shining through*
> *Life begins anew.*
> *Ayea, Ayea, Ayea!*

SUMMER SOLSTICE SPELL: JUNE 20–22

Midsummer's Eve, Midsummer Solstice, Fae Day, Litha, Letha's Day

Magic altar decorations: A silver or gold altar cloth, fruit (such as apples, apricots, and oranges), feathers, and seasonal flowers.

As the sun rises on the morning of the Summer Solstice, legend has it that the "Shining One" dresses in a robe of bird feathers and walks along the ancient stone avenue called "Callanish" on the Isle of Lewis in the Outer Hebrides. The cuckoo, the magical bird of Tir na

N'Og (Celtic Otherworld), heralds the Shining One's, the sun's, arrival on this, the brightest and longest day of the year.

Midsummer's Eve is a time to give respect to the faeries and other magical creatures. Gifts of food and drink are left out for the faeries, and the feast includes otherworldly favorites such as milk, honey, and sweets. Help is given and received between mortals and faeries on this day, as it is the ideal day to form new alliances with the fae and communicate with them.

Fresh flowers
A chalice of water
A mortar and pestle
3 pinches of dried lavender flowers
3 pinches of dried rose petals
3 pinches of dried jasmine flowers
A bowl
A silver bell
Your magic wand

Casting the Spell

The purpose of this spell is to attract helpful faeries and their magical gifts. Before you cast this spell, use your mortar and pestle to grind the lavender, rose, and jasmine flowers into a fine powdery faery dust. As you grind the ingredients, chant:

Lavender, rose, and jasmine flowers
Draw the fae here on this magic hour!

Imagine being in a magical garden surrounded by helpful and friendly faeries. Put the faery dust in the bowl. Hold the bowl upward between your hands, and say three times:

By air, fire, water, and earth
Bring joy, magic, merriment, and mirth
By the friendly fae, so be it!

Take the bowl of faery dust, the fresh flowers, the bell, and the chalice filled with water outdoors, somewhere private, just before sunset on Midsummer's Eve. Put half of the fresh flowers in the trees or flower bushes nearby. Create a faery ring by tying a loop on each end of a nine-foot cord. Put your athame tip through one loop, and stick your athame in the earth where you want the center of the circle to be. Put your index finger of your power hand through the loop on the opposite end of the cord and gently stretch it out. Holding the cord taut, you should walk clockwise in a circle, dragging the heel of your shoe to mark the circle outline. Walk clockwise around the circle again, and lay half of the fresh flowers on top of the circle outline. As you do this, say:

> *May the helpful faeries come into this ring at twilight*
> *May we merry meet and merry part, with blessings bright.*

Once your faery ring is drawn, create a faery magic circle by sprinkling water from your chalice clockwise all around the inside of the faery ring. Hold your wand in your power hand with the point outward; face the east direction of your faery ring and slowly spin in a clockwise circle. As you do this, imagine white light shooting out of your wand tip. Draw another circle of white light over the first circle. Stand at the center of the circle and say:

> *With this magic ring and circle of power*
> *I invite the friendly and helpful faeries*
> *Of air, fire, water, and earth to be here now*
> *And join me in the twilight of Midsummer's Eve*
> *Blessed be! Blessed be! Blessed be!*

Face east, and ring the bell with your power hand three times. Sprinkle some of the faery dust in the east quadrant, and say:

> *Fae of the air, sylphs, and sprites*
> *Please grant me the breath of life*
> *Nature fae of joy, magic, mirth, and merriment*
> *Please bless me with your gentle gifts.*

Face south and ring the bell three times. Sprinkle some faery dust in the south quadrant, and say:

> *Fae of the light, salamanders and newts*
> *Please grant me drive and creative fire*
> *Nature fae of joy, magic, mirth, and merriment*
> *Please bless me with your gentle gifts.*

Face west, and ring the bell three times. Sprinkle some faery dust in the west quadrant, and say:

> *Fae of the water, nymphs, undines, and merpeople*
> *Please grant me deep emotions and feelings*
> *Nature fae of joy, magic, mirth, and merriment*
> *Please bless me with your gentle gifts.*

Face north, and ring the bell three more times. Sprinkle the rest of the faery dust in the north quadrant, and say:

> *Fae of the earth, bright Sidhe, dwarfs, and gnomes*
> *Please grant me solidarity and stability*
> *Nature fae of joy, magic, mirth, and merriment*
> *Please bless me with your gentle gifts.*

Sit or stand quietly in the faery circle, and imagine the friendly fae of air, fire, water, and earth granting you magical gifts tonight, and every night. Spend at least an hour in the faery circle. When you are ready, ring the bell nine times. Thank the helpful faeries, and bid farewell to the elemental powers. Pull up the double circle of white light, and scatter the flowers in the faery ring. As you do, say:

> *Blessed fae, thank you for your gentle gifts.*

Use your foot to eradicate the outline of the faery circle. Leave the area as undisturbed and natural as possible. In the next week, plant some flowers and/or vegetables in your garden to honor the friendly fae.

LUGHNASSAD SPELL: AUGUST 1

Lammas

Magic altar decorations: A red, orange, rust, or gold altar cloth, berries, tree leaves, flowers, grains, nuts, vegetables, fruits, and corn dollies made from corn husks and ribbon.

Celebrated on the first week of August, *Lughnassad* means the wedding feast of Lugh, the Celtic sun God, to Rosemerta, the Rose Mother. *Nassad* means "to give in marriage." Associated with the lion and Leo, this is a time to celebrate the setting sun and the ascendancy of the moon. Lugh possesses many magical treasures and is extremely generous. He is the God who possesses mastery over all the arts and crafts. He is also the deliverer and wizard king of the mythological Tuatha de Danann.

A picnic of cakes, fruits,   Sunshine water
   vegetables, nuts, and   12 stones
   homemade bread

CASTING THE SPELL

The purpose of this spell is to empower yourself and those you love with the warmth and light of the sun. On the day before Lughnassad, make some sunshine water by filling a clear glass jar with spring or well water. Hold the jar in your hands, and say:

> *Mighty Lugh, divine sun God so bright*
> *Please fill this water with your empowering light.*

Put the jar out in the sun for at least three hours to empower it with divine solar energies. Fill sports bottles with the water to take with you on your picnic. On Lughnassad, take the day off and go on a lazy, tasty, magical picnic. It is a great way to empower yourself and those you love. Find a sweet spot outdoors in a natural environment, somewhere that you treasure. Bring plenty of food and water, utensils, napkins, bottle opener, and ice. As you set up your picnic, before you begin eating, make a toast by raising your glasses filled with sunshine water, and say:

> Blessed be the divine sun
> Blessed be all those who are gathered here
> May the God and Goddess bless, guide, and protect us all!

Take your time, and enjoy your picnic. Explore the area. As you do, gather together twelve small stones and place them in a circle around your picnic area. As the sun sets, say:

> Blazing, sacred sun, thank you for shining upon us
> In this time and in all times
> In this place and in all places
> On this day and on all days
> Please empower us with your divine light
> Bless us with your creative fire
> Thank you warm and constant friend. Blessed be!

When your picnic and blessing have been completed, return any food scraps and leftover beverages into the earth before you leave in honor of the Celtic God of mastery, Lugh. Take one of the stones with you to remind you of your empowering day. Be sure to leave the area in a divine, trash-free state.

AUTUMNAL EQUINOX SPELL: SEPTEMBER 20–22

Mabon, Harvest Home, Hellith's Day, Ingathering, and Fomhair

Magic altar decorations: An orange or brown altar cloth, filled cornucopias, shafts of wheat and grasses, acorns, breads, cakes, vegetables, nuts, and fruits of the harvest.

On this witch and wizard sabbat, day and night are equal. Essentially a mirrored image of the Spring Equinox, the Autumnal Equinox celebrates the season's harvest and begins the necessary process of collecting seeds for the next growing cycle. It is also a time for reflection, meditation, creation of balance in your life, and healing.

A white candle   A white feather
Pachouli oil   A white stone

CASTING THE SPELL

The purpose of this spell is to send healing angel light to someone you love. Cast this spell after sunset on the eve of this witch and wizard sabbat. Draw a magic circle of white light, and call in the elemental powers. Dress the candle with the scented oil, and then anoint yourself. Wipe any remaining oil from your hands. Light the candle, and say three times:

> *Bright light, candlelight*
> *Bring the angels here tonight.*

Gently hold the feather in your receiving hand, and hold the stone in your power hand. Focus your awareness on the person you are sending healing angel light to. Turn your mind completely to the magical work at hand, and direct positive thoughts toward the person receiving the angel light. Gaze at the candlelight, or its reflection, for a few minutes. All the while, think of the person you are sending healing energy to.

In your mind's eye, imagine an enormous flock of angels before you. Shape your angels to suit your needs. They can be bright balls of white light, divine beings with soft downy feathers, larger-than-life and powerful; or magical creatures with faerylike wings. Take a few deep breaths to build your focus and power, and imagine sending the enormous group of angels before you directly to the person you want to send healing light to. Ask the angels to shower the person with divine light and healing energy. Imagine the angels doing exactly that for a few minutes. When you are done, thank the angels, bid farewell to the elemental powers, and pull up the circle. Keep the feather on your altar for at least twenty-one days. Return the stone to nature. As you do so, say three times:

Thank you, divine angels for your healing light.

PART III

THE THIRTEEN WITCH AND WIZARD ESBATS

THE WITCH AND WIZARD ESBATS are the high moons. They signal a time of instincts, intuition, imagination, and receptivity. Moonlight acts as a regulator of the human body, which is made up of approximately 70 percent water. The moon influences our emotions in a similar way as it does the rising and ebbing of the ocean tides. Aspiring and practicing witches and wizards wisely use the tremendous lunar power of the high moons to cast spells and attain magical goals.

1ST ESBAT—WOLF MOON SPELL

The first witch and wizard esbat is called the wolf moon. Many of us have, or have had, a special friendship with animal companions, whether cat, wolf, owl, bear, or the magical phoenix and dragon. Moving out to the woods of northern California, I had the experience of being around wolf hybrids that were part dog, but mostly wolf. These incredible animal companions helped me to better understand not only human nature but the energies of the wolf moon as well.

The first esbat is the first full moon after the Winter Solstice. As the cycle of light shifts and the days grow longer, it becomes a time for knowing your primal and wild self. The wolf, eagle, dolphin, dragon, cat, rat, and phoenix, each represents aspects of your primal self and your connection to the whole of Oneness. Your primal self is the basis of who you are within your inner reaches without any of the exterior "sugar coating." From time to time you need to run with the wolves, fly with the eagles, and swim with the dolphins in order to get in touch with your wild nature while at the same time reaffirming the whole of who you are.

A picture or object signifying your animal totem	A white candle
	A drum
A green candle	Cedar oil

CASTING THE SPELL

The purpose of this spell is to tap into the natural power of your wild self and your animal helpers. If possible cast this spell at ten in the evening or at the exact time of the full moon. (*Note:* Many calendars note the time of the full moon or use an ephemeris.) If it is impossible for you to cast this spell at the specified time, make every effort to cast it as close to the full moon as you can. Begin by rubbing both the green and white candles with the cedar oil. As you do so, go over in your mind what you want from this spell. What do you want the energy of your animal self and helpers to be directed toward? In magic your expectation and intention should always be clear. The clearer your expectation, the better your chance of actually getting what you desire. Insert the candles into their appropriate holders, and place the picture or object signifying your animal totem between the two candles. Pound the drum nine times. Light the green candle, and repeat this invocation from the Nordic Kalevala:

> *The cold told me a tale*
> *The rain blew me some poems:*
> *Another tale came to me in the winds,*
> *Carried by the swell of the sea;*
> *Birds added words,*
> *The treetops, sentences.*

Merge with the candlelight, and say in a firm voice:

> *Sacred powers of nature*
> *Divine energy of my totem,*
> *Come into my circle of light.*

Light the white candle, and say:

> *Sacred powers of nature*
> *Divine energy of Oneness*
> *Come into my circle of light.*

Take up the drum and begin at the north point of the circle. Facing north, pound the drum three times, and then say aloud:

> *Element of Earth,*
> *Give my magic birth.*

Pound the drum three more times, and then say:

> *Element of Earth,*
> *You are all I'm worth.*

Pound the drum three times while imagining all the properties of earth, including stability, solidness, fertility, and the like. Move to the east point of the circle, and facing east, pound the drum three times, and then say aloud:

> *Element of Air,*
> *Give my magic life.*

Pound the drum three more times, and say:

> *Element of Air,*
> *Fly high like a kite.*

Pound the drum three more times while envisioning the powers of air—including flexibility, expansion, vitality, and the like—entering your being. Walk clockwise around the circle three times. Pound the drum nine times more. When you have finished, bid farewell to the elements, and pull up the circle. Allow the candles to burn down safely. In the next week, do something to help Mother Nature, for example, write a check and send it to an Earth-friendly charity, plant a tree, or pick up garbage at a local park.

2ND ESBAT—STORM MOON SPELL

The second full moon after the Winter Solstice, the Storm Moon, signifies a time of the year when the many faces of winter storms show themselves to the world. At times they can be fearsomely destructive while overall being positive and nurturing. The water that these storms leave behind after the spring thaw can be vital to plant and animal life. The storms generated at this time often set a tone for the whole year.

Times when there are lots of storms and water are called "wet years," and times there are few storms and water are called "dry years." Water is a basic element of life, representing fluidity and change. The root of the word *storm* means "to stir," and the natural powers of storms really can stir things up, causing permanent change in your surroundings and in your life—sometimes for the better, sometimes not.

You may not be dramatically rescued by a giant while hiding in a stone hovel on a wind-and-rain-swept island—as was Harry Potter in J. K. Rowling's, *Harry Potter and the Sorcerer's Stone*—but you can use the power of the Storm Moon to stir your life in a positive way.

During this time, when the magical waters of life are being stirred, the vibrancy of the high moon can readily move and stir you into action.

A green candle

A red candle

A white candle

A pen or quill

Lavender oil

A sage-and-cedar smudge stick

A quartz crystal

A cup of water

CASTING THE SPELL

The purpose of this spell is to help you understand that you have choices and that you can significantly influence the direction of your life in constructive, positive ways. Cast this spell at 11 P.M. or, if possible, after dark at the exact time of the full moon. Many witches and wizards already have magic names, to be used when practicing magic and casting spells. If you do not have a magic name, select a name that you have always liked, perhaps a name from mythology or one from nature. Wash the quartz crystal and set it aside for now. Use the pen or quill to inscribe your magic name in runes on each of the candles. Refer to the Runes in appendix C in this book and their alphabetic correspondences. Rub a thin coat of lavender oil over the candles. Anoint yourself, and wipe any remaining oil from your hands. Put the white candle in the center of your altar. Place the green (Goddess) candle to its left and the red (God) candle to its right. Light the white candle, and say:

> *I am [say your magic name]*
> *By the sacred light of the white flame*
> *I am empowered by my magic name*
> *As I will, so shall it be!*

Light the green candle from the white candle, and repeat:

> *I am [say your magic name]*
> *By the sacred light of the green flame*

I am empowered by my magic name
As I will, so shall it be!

Light the red candle from the green one, and repeat:

I am [say your magic name]
By the sacred light of the red flame
I am empowered by my magic name
As I will, so shall it be!

Light the smudge. Carefully bathe the crystal in the smudge smoke for a few minutes. Sit or stand with the crystal in your power hand, and ponder a couple of choices you need to make in the near future. Imagine making the best possible choices. Set that image, that sensation, into the stone by inhaling and then pulsing your breath sharply out of your nostrils. Repeat this process three times. As you do this, imagine setting the image of you making the best possible choices in the near future into the crystal with the power of your focused thought. Gently put the crystal into the water, and invoke the spirit of the water by saying:

Spirit of water, rain, hail, ice, and snow
Help me to make the best choices possible.
Please guide, bless, and nourish me.
May the divine powers of the water element
Now fill this crystal stone!

Using the crystal point stir the water clockwise, very slowly, for several minutes. As you do, chant:

Help me to make the best possible choices.

Cover the crystal in lavender oil. As you do, chant,

Help me to make the best possible choices.

Hold the stone in your receiving hand, and imagine easily and wisely making the best possible choices you can make in the near future. Step through the window to the future, and be there for a few minutes, making those excellent, empowering choices. Continue this visualization for at least fifteen minutes. When you have finished, bid farewell to the elemental powers, and pull up the circle. Allow the candles to burn down safely. Put the crystal on your altar, or if you like, you can hold it in your receiving hand while you dream.

3RD ESBAT—CHASTE MOON SPELL

The Chaste Moon symbolizes purity. *Chaste* derives its meaning from the Latin word *castus*, meaning "pure." Virtuous words matched with virtuous actions and joined with clear intentions symbolize the energy of the third witch and wizard esbat.

As the third full moon of the cycle, the Chaste Moon also represents the energy of the Trinity. The threefold Trinity carries many meanings. Trinity embraces the union of three parts or elements into one. The phases of the moon reflect the triple aspects of creation, destruction, and regeneration within nature, and the merging of the three into One.

A keyboard, guitar, or other musical instrument	Nag Champra incense or your favorite kind

CASTING THE SPELL

The purpose of this spell is to seek your highest potential in body, mind, and spirit. Cast it at exactly nine in the evening at the time of the full moon, or as close to this time as you can manage it. The spell draws on the natural harmony of the musical fifth. The fifth is the strongest musical relationship. It is deemed "perfect," because it has no major or minor quality. It is the purest sound, like going home! Draw a magic sphere of white light around the area in front of which you are standing, and step into it. Call in the elemental powers. Light the incense, and say:

> *C, E, F, G, A, and B, sing to me*
> *North, east, south, west, above and below*

Please help me attain my highest potential
So be it! Blessed be!

Face north, and play a C note. Say:

One, two, three, four, five
Bring my highest potential alive!

Face east, and play an E note. Say:

One, two, three, four, five
Bring my highest potential alive!

Face south, and play an F note, and say:

One, two, three, four, five
Bring my highest potential alive!

Face west, and play a G note, and say,

One, two, three, four, five
Bring my highest potential alive!

Look below, and play an A note. Say:

As below, so above me
Inspire me! Blessed be!

Look above, and play a B note. Say:

As above, so below me
Inspire me! Blessed be!

Face your altar, and play C, E, F, G, A, and B notes, in that order. Say:

C, E, F, G, A, and B, sweet harmony
North, east, south, west, above and below
Please empower, bless, and inspire me.
So be it! Blessed be!

Play some of your favorite tunes for a while, and imagine attaining your highest potential. Enjoy the experience! When you have finished, bid farewell to the elements, step out of the sphere of light, and pull it up.

4TH ESBAT—SEED MOON SPELL

The fourth witch and wizard esbat, the Seed Moon, is the time for sowing magical patterns and planting the seeds for the future. You probably will not be transplanting magical screaming mandrake seedlings, as did the students in J. K. Rowling's *Harry Potter and the Chamber of Secrets*. At the same time, regardless of what you decide to grow, you have to select seeds or seedlings, plant them, water and cultivate them, give them plenty of sunlight, and encourage them to grow to fruition.

Metaphorically, seeds are things you are continually planting in order to stay ahead of the progression of life. They are the "seed-corn" receptacles from which life lays dormant and then emerges in its infinite variety. Every spell, too, is akin to a seed, as it contains and initiates an energy that attempts to manifest itself. This is a basic premise of magic. The better you are at gathering, directing, merging, and manifesting this magical energy, the greater your power as a witch or wizard.

A green candle
A flowerpot filled with earth
A package of white flower
  seeds (any easy-to-grow
  annual)

A chalice of water
Your magic wand

CASTING THE SPELL

The purpose of this spell is to plant, cultivate, and harvest one of your magical goals. Cast it at 8 P.M., or, if possible, after dark at the exact time of the full moon. Select a goal that you would like to manifest. Make sure it is something that you know is possible to attain. Draw a magic circle, and call in the elemental powers. Light the candle, and say three times:

Blessed be the Seed Moon!

Pour the seeds out of the package and into your power hand. Empower them by merging with Oneness and saying three times:

Blessed be these magic seeds!

Put the seeds in the soil in the flowerpot according to the planting instructions. As you plant the seeds, chant:

Magic seeds, sprout, grow, and thrive
Please bring my magic goal alive!

Hold your magic wand over the flowerpot, and move it in three clockwise circles around the rim. As you do, say:

Magic seeds, one, two, three
Blessed be! Blessed be! Blessed be!

Hold the chalice of water in your hands, and empower it by merging with Oneness, and saying:

Blessed be this nourishing water!

Slowly water the seeds. As you do, repeat three times:

Magic seeds, sprout, grow, and thrive
Please bring my magic goal alive!

Imagine the seeds sprouting, growing, and thriving. Now imagine your magic goal coming to fruition. Once again, hold your wand in your power hand over the flowerpot, and move it in three clockwise circles around the rim. As you do, repeat:

Magic seeds, one, two, three
Blessed be! Blessed be! Blessed be!

Continue imagining your magic goal coming to fruition as the flowers in the pot sprout, grow, and thrive. Continue this visualization for at least fifteen minutes. When you have finished, bid farewell to the elemental powers, and pull up the circle. Put the flowerpot where it will get plenty of sunlight and attention. Be sure to tend it daily. When you water your seeds and then your seedlings and then your young plants, repeat each time:

Please bring my magic goal alive!

5TH ESBAT—HARE MOON SPELL

The fifth esbat, the Hare Moon, attracts the good luck and abundance of the hare. North American Algonquian tribes credit the hare with forming the Earth, then ordering and enlarging it. In many Trickster tales, a humanlike hare, called Great Hare or White Hare, acts as a masterful magician. Quick to adapt to its environment, the hare has the ability to multiply its numbers very quickly. This ability helps it to thrive within nature.

The Hare Moon heralds the abundant beauty and bounty of spring. One way to draw the magical powers of this high moon to you is to put up a hummingbird feeder. Many native North American plants depend on hummingbirds for pollination. Hummingbirds fly in a giant U-shaped pattern, much like an elongated half-moon. They can fly backwards and upside down at impressive speeds. Similar to those of faeries, hummingbird wings rotate at the shoulder, allowing these tiny birds to make a forward stroke immediately followed by a backward stroke so that they can hover and change course at will.

A green candle
A pen or quill
Rose-scented oil
A hummingbird feeder (small, empty milk carton, red wire or red pipe cleaner)

Hummingbird nectar potion
red paper, red ribbons, and red flowers

CASTING THE SPELL

The purpose of this spell is to attract good luck and abundance. Cast it after dark, if possible at the exact time of the full moon. Draw a magic circle and call in the elemental powers. Use the pen or quill to inscribe the words *Good Luck* and *Abundance* on the candle body. Dress the candle with the scented oil and anoint yourself. Wipe any remaining oil from your hands, and light the candle. Say:

> *Bright candlelight bring to me*
> *By earth, air, light, and sea*
> *Abundance, good luck, and prosperity*
> *By the light of the moon, blessed be!*

Purchase or make a hummingbird feeder. To make one, you can use a small, clean milk carton. Make a hole in the upper section, large enough for a toothpick to fit through. Decorate the outside of the carton with red paper, red ribbons, and red flowers. Hold the feeder between your hands, and empower it by merging with Oneness, and saying:

> *Sweet hummingbirds, winged fae*
> *Sacred flower kissers of spring*
> *She, with her necklace of colored spots*
> *He, with his flashing, jeweled throat*
> *As you breathe, fly, hover, and feed*
> *Please bring me good luck, abundance, and prosperity*
> *By earth, air, light, and sea, blessed be!*

Take a few deep breaths, and merge with the candlelight or its reflection. Imagine beautiful hummingbirds flying into your life and bringing with them a bounty of good luck, abundance, and prosperity. Step into the future for a few minutes, and enjoy the feeling of plenty! Expand this visualization for at least fifteen minutes. When you have finished, bid farewell to the elemental powers and pull up the circle. The next morning, fill the feeder with homemade hummingbird nectar potion. Boil 1 part sugar to 4 parts water (1 cup water with ¼ cup sugar). Never use honey or red food coloring, as these will harm or poison the humming birds. Stir the potion until it cools. As you stir it, chant:

Good luck, abundance, and prosperity, fly to me
On the wings of the hummingbirds
As I will, so shall it be.

Pour the potion into the feeder. Repeat:

Good luck, abundance, and prosperity, fly to me
On the wings of the hummingbirds
As I will, so shall it be.

Hang your feeder in a shady, calm location, within fifteen feet of tall trees, vines, or dense bushes. Use red wire or a red pipe cleaner to hang it. After you hang the feeder, repeat,

Good luck, abundance, and prosperity, fly to me
On the wings of the hummingbirds
As I will, so shall it be.

Wash out the feeder and replace the nectar potion every two days in hot weather. Repeat the chant each time you do this to draw more and more good luck, abundance, and prosperity into your life. Hummingbirds eat insects, as many as four hundred or five hundred per day—and even more in rainy weather—so garden organically whenever possible. As you watch the hummingbirds feed, take joy in life, encourage love, and be open to nature's beauty and bounty. Draw the natural abundance of spring to you as you watch your feathered friends. Leave the feeder up at least three weeks after seeing the last hummingbird of the season.

6th Esbat—Dyad Moon Spell

The sixth esbat is the Dyad Moon. In alchemy, 6 is considered a perfect number, since it can be represented as $1 + 2 + 3 = 6$. In numerology, it is the number of home and family. The word *dyad* stems from the Greek and Latin word *dyas*, meaning "the number two." In numerology, 2 is the number of partnership and positive combinations. Accordingly, the Dyad Moon provides the perfect night for working on positive, creative combinations, a time of productive teamwork on the physical, mental, and spiritual planes of experience.

The Dyad Moon symbolizes the strengthening force of working in tandem with your allies, be they mortal or spiritual. It is often easier to work, play, and love, when those you do so with balance and enhance your abilities. When you work in rapport with the divine, be it God, Goddess, the Great Spirit, Oneness (however you refer to this power), it becomes possible to balance and intensify your magical abilities. At the time of this Boon Moon, you can step through the divine door of opportunity and commune with the Goddess. Cherish her gift as you would cherish the sacred land, the Mother Earth.

A silver or gold ring	White sage smudge
2 white candles	Honeysuckle-scented oil
A pen or quill	

CASTING THE SPELL

The purpose of this spell is to ask the Goddess to grant you a gift, or boon. It is an ancient method for igniting your powers of creativity. Use a ring that you will want to wear or carry for the next year and a day. It can be a ring that you already have or it can be a new one. (For an extra magical touch, have a jeweler inscribe *Divine Boon* inside the ring band.) Cast this spell at midnight. Draw a magic circle and call in the elemental powers. Knock nine times on the altar, in three series of three. Inscribe the words *Divine Boon* on both candles with the pen or quill. Dress both candles with a thin coat of honeysuckle oil. Anoint yourself with the oil, and wipe any remaining oil from your hands. As you light each of the candles, repeat:

> *Boon Goddess, Lady of the summer night,*
> *Dressed and blessed in starry white light*
> *Please shower me with your silvery moon beams*
> *And open the divine door of opportunity*
> *By the silver White Lady, blessed be!*

Light the smudge. Carefully bathe the ring in the smudge smoke for a few minutes. As you smudge the ring, chant,

On this Dyad Moon, Goddess please bless me with your boon.

Slide the ring onto one finger of your receiving hand. Face north, and say:

I am [state your magical name].
Great Goddess, I pray that you will grant me a boon.

A boon comes because of your good works. Take a few minutes to think about the good things you have done in the past year. Merge with the candlelight, and say:

Dear Goddess, blessed White Lady
I have done these good works in the past.
[State your good works aloud to the Goddess.]
You have seen my honest efforts and loving intentions.
Please Great Goddess, grant me a boon of divine creativity
Praise to you, Lady! Blessed be, Great Goddess!
Blessed be! Blessed be! Blessed be!

Hold up your hand with the boon ring on it, and say:

With this ring,
I unite with the divine powers of creativity!
Blessed be! Blessed be! Blessed be!

Continue gazing at the candlelight, and merge with the divine source, with Oneness. Imagine your creative abilities growing stronger and stronger. Imagine going deep into a magical well and pulling up ideas and creative thoughts. Continue visualizing this for at least fifteen minutes, noting ideas and thoughts that come to you in your Book of Shadows. When you have finished merging with your source, bow nine times toward the altar in honor of the Goddess. Center yourself and knock three times on the altar. Thank the Goddess, bid farewell to the elemental powers, and pull up the circle. Allow the candles to burn down safely. Review your notes in your Book of Shadows over the next couple of days, and use the information in a constructive, creative way. Wear or carry the ring for at least a year and a day to encourage renewed, inspired creativity.

7TH ESBAT—MEAD MOON SPELL

A moon symbolic of etheric harmony, lunar fertility, and lucid dreams, the seventh witch and wizard esbat is called the Mead Moon. One of the first known fermented beverages, the honeywine called "mead," is thought to be the sacred drink of the ancient Teutonic gods. It is made of honey and water, to which malt, yeast, and spices can be added to create the spiced mead called "metheglin," which means "healing liquor."

Odin, the Norse Father God of wisdom, is known for his insatiable thirst for knowledge and almost lost his life while trying to obtain a drink of magically imbued mead. Odin's mead is the mead of poetic inspiration. It is said that whoever drinks this liquid becomes a poet and all-knower of magic, runes, and charms. The meadlike potion you will make in this esbat spell will not necessarily transform you into a great poet, a power animal, or another person, but it will help you to transform your life by finding answers to your questions so that you can more easily attain your dreams.

Your magic wand	A moonstone
Chamomile-and-lavender tea	Rosemary-scented oil
3 teaspoons of honey	Book of Shadows
A melon	A pen

CASTING THE SPELL

The purpose of this spell is to find the answer to one question by using dream incubation magic. Cast it just before you go to sleep. Take about fifteen minutes to think about one question, something you have a strong desire to answer and resolve right now. Think about all the aspects of the question, every nuance, every nook and cranny. Draw a magic circle, and call in the elementals. Draw a half-moon of white energy light at each of the four quarters with your wand. Prepare a cup of the chamomile-and-lavender tea (made from packaged tea bags or loose herbs). Sweeten the tea with the honey. As you slowly stir in the honey, chant over and over:

Bring me an answer in my dreams. Blessed be!

Cut the melon into pieces. Eat the melon and sip the relaxing tea. Between bites and sips, say:

Answer, please come to me in my dreams. So be it!

When you are finished with the tea and melon, rub a thin coat of rosemary-scented oil into the moonstone. (Rosemary is also known as elf leaf.) As you anoint the stone, say:

Magical moonstone and oil of elf leaf
Bring an answer in my dreams
Empower and inform me
So be it! Blessed be!

Anoint yourself with the scented oil, and repeat:

Magical oil of elf leaf
Bring an answer in my dreams
Empower and inform me
So be it! Blessed be!

Leave the circle open. As you drift to sleep, holding the moonstone in your receiving hand, repeat over and over:

Magical moonstone, please bring an answer in my dreams
And I will remember, blessed be!

Hold the moonstone in your hand as you sleep. In the morning, write down what you recall of your dreams. When you have finished, bid farewell to the elemental powers and pull up the circle and half-moons of light.

8TH ESBAT—WORT MOON SPELL

The Wort Moon is a catalyst for transformation. *Wort* stems from the Old English *wyrt*, meaning "root" or "plant." Today's wort is usually a type of plant or herb, for example, liverwort, St. John's wort, or pennywort. In beer brewing, the infusion of malted barley combined with hops and other specialty grains produces another sort of wort: this one, when combined with the yeast organism, ferments and springs to life.

Your full potential is also waiting to spring to life. Fulfilling your potential depends on what and how you think about yourself and your life. The quality of your thoughts determines the quality of your life. This Wort Moon Spell helps you to focus on what you want, rather than on what you do not. It encourages you to express yourself and your feelings positively, find meaning and purpose in life, love and be loved, accept yourself, enjoy each day, and remember to be flexible.

Lavender essential oil	A blue candle
Cedarwood essential oil	Sandalwood incense
3 bay leaves	A dark-colored stone
3 pinches of St. John's wort	from nature

CASTING THE SPELL

The purpose of this spell is to transform one negative thing in your life into a positive one. Cast it at midnight on the esbat. Fill your tub with warm water for a ritual bath. If you prefer, you can shower, putting the oils and bay leaves in a shower glove or washcloth. Tear the bay leaves, and add them to the bathwater, along with nine drops of the lavender oil and three drops of the cedarwood oil. As you do this, say:

Sacred plants, now empower me
Please grant me the ability
To change this negativity

Into blessed positivity.
As I will, so shall it be!

When you have finished bathing, towel off and get dressed. Face your altar, and draw a magic circle. Draw a blazing star of cobalt blue light inside the magic circle. Call in the elemental powers. Sprinkle the St. John's wort over your altar. Light the candle, dedicating it by saying:

I dedicate this sacred light to positive change.

Light the incense from the candle flame. As you do, say:

I dedicate this sacred incense to positive change.

Hold the stone in your power hand. In your mind's eye, imagine the one negative thing that you want to be rid of. Say three times in a strong, firm voice:

Stone of nature's energy
Take this negativity from me.
So be it! Blessed be!

Rub the lavender oil on the stone for a few minutes. As you do, chant:

Negativity go from me, positivity flow to me.

Imagine stepping into the future and that the transformation from negative to positive has already taken place. Immerse yourself so deeply in this positive future that all else falls away. Completely turn your mind toward what you want and away from what you do not want. Imagine yourself positively expressing your thoughts and feelings, finding meaning and purpose in life, and loving and being loved. You are learning to accept yourself, to enjoy each day, and remembering to be flexible. Enjoy this positive glimpse of the future. Be there with your imagination, enjoying all the benefits of this positive transformation. Continue this visualization for at least thirty minutes, and then when you feel the time is right, bid farewell to the elemental powers, and pull up the blazing star and magic circle. Allow the candle to burn down safely. Take the stone outside, and bury it in the ground. As you bury it, repeat:

> *Negativity go from me, positivity flow to me.*

9TH ESBAT—BARLEY MOON SPELL

The Barley Moon represents the magical balance of nature and the aspects of birth, growing, maturing, resurrection, and rebirth. It is traditionally a Harvest Moon, except in the years when there are thirteen esbats.

Pliny the Elder, Roman scholar in the first century C. E., said that barley with its triple spikelets is the oldest of foods. Barley is associated with the Greek goddess Demeter. Like the corn mother, the barley mother symbolizes the never-ending and continually renewing cyclic aspects of nature.

Your athame	A green candle
A bowl of barley grain	A green notebook
A piece of malachite	A green felt or gel pen

CASTING THE SPELL

The purpose of this spell is to become more successful. Cast it just after dark or, if possible, at the exact time of the full moon. Draw a magic circle. Then draw a Witches' Pyramid, an energetic pyramid of white light, with your athame, cutting the base or foundation first. As you do this, say:

> *With the powers of the element of earth*
> *I am the foundation of the pyramid*
> *I know, I think, I learn, I question.*

Cut the right wall of the pyramid next. As you do, say:

> *With the powers of the element of air*
> *I am the right, the might*
> *I will, I intend, I create, I exemplify.*

Cut the left wall of the pyramid, and say:

> *With the powers of the element of fire*
> *I am the left, the flame*
> *I dare, I merge, I use my power wisely.*

Cut another circle of white light on top of the original circle you drew. As you do, say:

> *With the powers of the element of water*
> *I am that which surrounds all things*
> *I keep silent, I wait patiently, I attain success.*

Light the candle. Hold the malachite in your power hand, merge with the stone, and say:

> *Mother and Father of the winds, waters, fires, and earth*
> *Lady and Lord of the stars, moon, planets, and universe*
> *I know this to be true without untruth.*
> *That which is below is one with that which is above.*
> *That which is above is one with that which is below.*
> *All things are and come from Oneness.*
> *By the sun and moon, the Lord and Lady*
> *By the star, seed corn, infant, and child*
> *May the wind and fire carry the power of success to me.*
> *May the water and earth nourish and nurture my success.*
> *By Mind, Matter, and Spirit, I am thrice blessed!*
> *Blessed be! Blessed be! Blessed be!*

Take out your green notebook, and set the malachite above it. Write down exactly what you want your success to be like. Be specific. Jot down those deep desires you have for a home, career, and family life. Go ahead and be bold and dare to create a brilliant image of your success. Continue writing for at least thirty minutes. When you have finished, thank the Goddess and God, and pull up the Witches' Pyramid and circle in the reverse order that you laid them. Carry the malachite with you to encourage blessed success.

10TH ESBAT—WINE MOON SPELL

Witches and wizards toast and celebrate love and fruition on the Wine Moon, the time of the final harvest. Traditionally, the better the harvest, the better the wine and celebration. The wine cup rests at the center of the altar and symbolizes the Goddess, divine love, the blood of life, and rebirth.

- A white candle
- A sheet of stationery or a greeting card
- A red pen
- A bottle of wine or sparkling cider
- A book of love poems
- Patchouli oil
- A 9-inch piece of gold ribbon
- An 8-inch piece of silver ribbon

CASTING THE SPELL

The purpose of this spell is to celebrate romance, love, and passion. Cast it after 9 P.M., or sometime after dark at the exact time of the full moon. Draw a magic circle, and call in the elemental powers. Dress the candle with a thin film of patchouli oil, anoint yourself, and wipe any remaining oil from your hands. Light the candle, and say:

Blessed be the sacred light of love.

On the paper or greeting card, use the red pen to write all the loving things you have always wanted to say to your beloved. Write the words that come straight from your heart. Go ahead and be bold! Set the paper or card aside for now. Carefully and quickly run the ribbons through the candle flame without burning them. The gold and silver ribbons symbolize the male and female powers. Rub a bit of the scented oil on the ribbons, let them dry, and braid them together knotting them at both ends. Put the ribbons inside the card or paper. Fold the paper in half. Then put the card or folded paper into the book of poems, marking the page of your favorite love poem, one that reflects your feelings for your beloved. Hold the book of poems between your hands, and empower it by saying:

I empower this book of poems
With the divine loving powers
Of the Goddess and God
With romance, love, and passion.
With this book of love
I draw my beloved to me.
So be it! Blessed be!

Hold the bottle of wine in your hands, and empower it by saying:

I empower this wine
With the divine loving powers
Of the Goddess and God
With romance, love, and passion.
With this wine of life
I draw my beloved to me.
The spell is done
We are two as one.

Give your beloved the book of poems and share the bottle of wine with him or her tonight. Anoint each other with the patchouli oil and enjoy a high moon of romance, love, and passion. When the night is over, bid farewell to the elemental powers, and pull up the circle.

11TH ESBAT—BLOOD MOON SPELL

The Blood Moon is the perfect night to get in touch with the power and wisdom of your ancestors by traveling through lifetimes. Blood is life, and it is most definitely thicker than water. The Old English word *blod* stems from the root that means "bloom," defined as "flourishing" or "vigorous." Concerning genetic memory, your blood, specifically the DNA in your blood, is like a mega filing system for ancestral wisdom and power.

If you imagine time to be circular instead of linear, then past lifetimes are actually simultaneous lifetimes. They only *seem* like past lifetimes due to our vantage point. Remote viewing works off this premise. In magic, you are more than one individual and more than one incarnation. You are like the eternal time traveler, with your power lying within your many lifetimes and experiences. All you have to do is access it.

A blue candle
Pictures of your ancestors
Amber resin or amber-scented
   oil

Frankincense incense
A strand of your hair
A red stone

CASTING THE SPELL

The purpose of this spell is to access the wisdom and power of your ancestors. If you do not know who your ancestors were, select a person from history that you greatly admire or feel a kinship with. Cast this spell at midnight, or if possible, at the exact time of the full Blood Moon. Draw a magic circle, and call in the elemental powers. Dress the candle with a thin film of the scented oil. Anoint yourself and the stone. Wipe any remaining oil from your hands. Light the candle, and say:

> *By the power of the Divine Mother and Father*
> *I respectfully ask for swift communication.*
> *Please grace me with the wisdom and power of my ancestors*
> *In the name of the Divine Mother and Father, so be it!*

Carefully burn the strand of your hair in the candle flame to call the spirits of your ancestors into the circle. Say:

> *I call my ancestors into this circle, right now!*

Light the incense from the candle flame, and say three times:

> *I am my ancestors*
> *My ancestors are me*
> *We are one.*

Sit back comfortably, and hold the stone in your receiving hand.
Close your eyes, and breathe gently and deeply. Relax your muscles
and let go of the tensions of the day. Now with each breath, imagine
moving back in time. Breathe in, and imagine yourself gently stepping into the picture of your ancestor. Imagine you are your ancestor for a few moments, and imagine looking out of your ancestor's
eyes at yourself. Once you can see a clear image of yourself from
your ancestor's eyes, you are in! Once you connect energetically with
your ancestor, merge with his or her spiritual essence. Continue to
breathe softly and rhythmically. In your mind's eye, look at what you
are wearing (or not wearing) as your ancestor would. Look at the
colors and fabrics of your clothes. Imagine moving around in your
ancestor's body. Observe your actions. Imagine looking at your surroundings. Perhaps you know what area you are in.

As you look around, start walking. You may become aware of
other people and other sounds around you, as well as of the animals
and plants. Continue to breathe rhythmically, using your breathing
to clarify the images and experience. Use the positive experiences
from your ancestor's vantage point to expand your mind. Allow yourself to absorb the wisdom of your ancestors energetically through
this experience. Take another deep breath. You feel relaxed and
empowered by your experience. Pay attention to your breathing for
a minute or so, and then step back into the present time and place.
Move your hands and feet. Look at the picture of your ancestor from
the vantage point of your own eyes. Clap your hands three times.
Set the stone on the altar. Whenever you want to access the wisdom
and power of your ancestors, hold the stone in your receiving hand,
and repeat three times:

I am my ancestors.
My ancestors are me.
We are one.

When you have finished, thank your ancestors, bid farewell to the elemental powers, and pull up the circle. Allow the candle to burn down safely.

12TH ESBAT—SNOW MOON SPELL

The winter brings with it the Snow Moon, the twelfth witch and wizard esbat. In the Cherokee tradition, White as Snow represents an elevated state of the soul. It is frozen water, such as snow, ice, and hail, that holds the potential of all things waiting to be manifested. With the heat of the sun and thaw, the unmanifested flows into the manifested. Just as with the practice of magic, it is as if you are awakened from a dream.

In the Norse runes, ice is represented as Isa (|), and it gives form and structure to primal creativity. Isa is a slow-moving force that is especially strong and can be represented, for example, by the movement of glaciers. Ice in the form of icebergs can be deadly, as it was in the case of the *Titanic*. Hail, like ice, is depicted in the runes as Hagalaz (ᚺ). Its alternate symbol form is (✳), which is the primal snowflake pattern. In this form, the six-fold Hagalaz is the Mother Rune, as all other runes can be formed from it. Hagalaz is a rune of transformation, change, evolution, merging, and protection. It represents the potential energy of crystallized patterns waiting to be manifested.

A holiday snow globe	A pen or quill
A white candle	Sandalwood incense
A purple candle	Your Book of Shadows

CASTING THE SPELL
The purpose of this spell is to foretell the patterns of the new year. Cast it at midnight. If possible, use a glass snow globe containing lots

of white "snow." Before you begin, write in your Book of Shadows one question about the coming year that you want answered. Also note the moon, date, and time. Draw a magic circle and draw a magic V of light. When drawing the V, stand in the middle of the circle, and imagine the Kenaz rune ($<$) surrounding you and forming the V enclosure as you turn around in a clockwise circle. Light the incense. Say:

> *Today flows into tomorrow*
> *Today flows into tomorrow*
> *Today flows into tomorrow*
> *The unmanifested flows into the manifested*
> *By the torch of Oneness, may I clearly see my future*
> *As I will, so shall it be!*

Use the pen or quill to inscribe the Isa ($|$) and Hagalaz (H) runes on the candles. Draw three of each of the runes on each of the candles, for a total of twelve runes. Dress the candles with a thin coat of sandalwood oil. Anoint yourself. Wipe any remaining oil from your hands, and light the candle. Say:

> *Isa, Isa, Isa, rune of form*
> *Strengthen my insight*
> *Hagalaz, Hagalaz, Hagalaz, rune of change*
> *Positively transform my life!*

Put the snow globe on a contrasting surface so that it can be easily viewed. Gaze at the globe for a minute or so. Pick up the globe and while you are holding it in your hands, say:

> *I empower this globe as a divine oracle.*

Shake the snow globe, and hold it so that it is illuminated in the candlelight. Study the globe. Watch the falling flakes. Get to know the nuances and details of the snow globe for about five minutes. Shake the globe, face north, and say:

> *The rune might is drawn 'round the sacred stead,*
> *Unwanted wights, wend away. Helpful spirits, stay!*

Face east, and repeat:

> *The rune might is drawn 'round the sacred stead,*
> *Unwanted wights, wend away. Helpful spirits, stay!*

Face south, and say:

> *The rune might is drawn 'round the sacred stead,*
> *Unwanted wights, wend away. Helpful spirits, stay!*

Face west, and repeat once again,

> *The rune might is drawn 'round the sacred stead,*
> *Unwanted wights, wend away. Helpful spirits, stay!*

Focus all your attention on the snow globe, and think about your question regarding the next year. Turn your mind completely toward your question. Read it out of your Book of Shadows, if you like. Shake the globe vigorously twelve times, stirring up the contents, while saying:

> *With great respect I call to you*
> *Urth, Verdandi, Skuld.*
> *Send the wisdom of the fates*
> *Through the snowy waters of time*
> *In this winter wonderland sphere*
> *Down the path of white beauty.*
> *Walk the wind of today and the dream of tomorrow*
> *So I may know the wisdom of the old ones*
> *And I will know the answer I seek*
> *I respectfully ask this of you. So mote it be!*

Continue to hold the globe between your hands, and turn your awareness completely to it. Turn the globe over a few times, and turn your mind to the water, snow, and images in the globe. Continue to ask the question about your future as you continue to observe the images in the globe. When you receive an answer or helpful images regarding your question, note them in your Book of Shadows. When you have finished, pull up the V enclosure and the magic circle in the reverse manner that you constructed them.

13TH ESBAT—OAK MOON SPELL

Because it does not occur every year, the 13th Esbat or Oak Moon is one of the most magical of all the moons. It draws on the power of the mighty oak, a tree of tremendous magical power; everything that grows on an oak is sacred. In stories, faeries, elves, and lovers meet and dance under the oaks. The sacred mistletoe also graces the oak. This 13th moon is a time to generate strength, endurance, success, and protection. It represents the completion of a cycle.

13 oak leaves	A green poster board
4 sprigs of mistletoe	Glue
A can of gold spray paint	Photos of yourself, your loved
Nag Champa incense (or your	ones, and pets
favorite kind)	A gold gel pen

CASTING THE SPELL

The purpose of this spell is to create a charm for happiness, love, and protection for yourself and your loved ones. The day before you cast this Oak Moon Spell, carefully spray paint the oak leaves and mistletoe sprigs gold. If you prefer, use a paint brush. Let the leaves and mistletoe dry overnight. Cast this spell at 11 P.M. or, if possible, at the exact time of the full moon. Draw a magic circle, and call in the elemental powers. Light the incense, and say:

> *All Mother and All Father, please hear my call*
> *May we be blessed by the grace of Goddess*
> *May we be blessed by the laughter of the Lord*

May we be guided by the hand of the gentle Lady
May we be guided by the creative light of God
May we be protected by the courage of the divine mother
May we be blessed by the strength of the divine father
Please fill our lives with love and happiness
By earth, air, fire, and sea, blessed be!

Stand in the center of your circle. In your mind's eye, imagine stepping into a magic castle of white crystal. Take a few deep, complete breaths and allow yourself to sense more details of the castle of light. Once you feel surrounded by the castle of light, you are ready to proceed. Glue the 13 oak leaves in a large circle on the green poster board. As you glue each leaf, say:

May we be blessed by the sacred power of the Oak.

Glue the mistletoe sprigs onto the poster board, one sprig at the top of the leaves, one at right side, one at the bottom, and one at the left side, in that order. As you glue each sprig, say:

May we be blessed by the sacred power of the Mistletoe.

Glue the photos of yourself, your love, your children, and all those people and pets that you love on the poster board. Select your favorite picture for the center of the leaf circle. Glue the others around the center picture and also, glue pictures on the outside of the circle of leaves so that the poster board is filled. As you glue each picture on, say:

May we be blessed by the powers of the Oak Moon.

Use the gold gel pen to write the words *happiness*, *love*, and *protection* around the edges of the pictures. Also use the pen to decorate the poster board with magic symbols such as stars, moons, and spirals. Put the poster board in front of you, and study it intensely. Merge with your creation, and say:

May our lives be filled with love and happiness
May we be blessed, guided, and protected.
I ask this with my heart, head, and spirit
By the Lord and Lady, blessed be!

Continue studying the poster board for at least fifteen minutes more. As you do, imagine your life and the lives of those you love being filled with happiness, love, joy, and laughter. Also imagine your loved ones as well as yourself being divinely protected from all harm. When you have finished, imagine stepping out of the castle of white light, bid farewell to the elements, and pull up the circle. Put the poster board somewhere where you will see it every day. When you look at it, turn your mind toward love, happiness, joy, and protection for those you love and yourself.

APPENDIX A

WITCH AND WIZARD
MAGIC STONES

The corresponding element and the spell-casting powers of witch
and wizard stones are as follows:

EARTH

Colors: Green, brown, gold, white,
and black stones

Amazonite Truth, luck, prosperity, success, growth, hope, faith,
inspiration, verbal skills, expression, creativity, psychic ability, and
receiving energy.

Black Tourmaline Ancestral communication, purification, protection, repels negative energy.

Cat's Eye Love magic, beauty, joy, boosts willpower, protection,
prosperity, riches, courage, good fortune, business success.

Chrysoprase Joy, good cheer, insight, creativity, fertility, wellness,
insight, brings out your magical potential, meditation, shapeshifting.

Emerald Psychic clarity, divination, growth, sexuality, healing, business success, inspiration, cleansing, cultivating patience, equilibrium
of body, mind, and spirit, meditation, wisdom, boosts the immune
system, love magic, attracts faeries and elves.

Green and Brown Agate   Courage, harmony, insight, balances emotions, vitality, abundance, prosperity, protection, truth, love magic.

Green Tourmaline   Regeneration, creativity, growth, healing, vitality, purification, divination, spirit guides, attracts faeries and elves.

Jet   Centering, protection, healing, divination, dream magic, good luck, mental strength, wisdom, psychic development.

Kunzite   Mental stability, balances body, mind, and spirit, love magic, joy, tolerance, releasing grief and unwanted memories, peace, boosts self-esteem.

Malachite   Strengthens will, communicates with nature, shapeshifting, divination, manifests goals, healing, prosperity, wealth, attracts faeries and elves.

Moldavite   Transformation, shapeshifting, metamorphosis, cleansing, meditation, expanding consciousness, motivation, accelerates change, attracts nature and garden spirits.

Moss Agate   Healing, joy, hope, happiness, longevity, strength, gardening stone, attracts faeries and elves.

Olivine   Love magic, fertility, joy, hope, good luck, protection, happiness, peace, harmony, beauty.

Peridot   Balance, healing, insight, clairvoyance, personal empowerment, clarity, enlightenment, stimulates tissue regeneration, boosts confidence.

Rock Quartz   Healing, balance, insight, clarity, expanded consciousness, meditation, divination, focus, concentration, manifestation, attracts nature spirits, power animals, spirit guides. Both crystals and the human body contain silicon. This forms the very real physical basis for our connection with quartz.

Turquoise   Starwalking, shapeshifting, timeshifting, endurance, healing, motivation, love magic, healing, compassion, beauty, ancestral knowledge, self-realization, attracts nature spirits.

AIR

Colors: Lavender, yellow, pastel blue, pastel pink, grey, and white stones

Fluorite Self-discipline, mental clarity, focus, peace, feminine empowerment, moon magic, love magic, out-of-body experience, dream magic.

Green Aventurine Good luck, creativity, divination, attracts adventures, opportunities, wealth, prosperity, increases imagination, improves eyesight, eye-opening stone, promotes growth, heals body, mind, and spirit, balances female and male energies, works as an excellent travel amulet.

Holey Stones Stones with holes in them are most always associated with the air element. Use them as doorways into the powers of air, into magical worlds, for example, the faery realms.

Pumice Mental clarity and agility, wisdom, knowledge, learning, focus, concentration, research, study, communication skills.

Staurolite (faery cross) Attracts nature spirits, divine messages, second sight, prosperity, abundance.

Tanzanite Truth, insight, divination, out-of-body experience, dream magic, expands consciousness, psychic development, shapeshifting.

FIRE

Colors: Red, orange, crimson, gold, white, brown, black, and banded stones

Amber Amber is actually fossilized resin. The Greeks called it "elektron," as it has electrical properties. Protection, love magic, magnetic attraction, stabilizes kundalini awakening, purification, insight, happiness, divination, attracts tree dryads.

Bloodstone   Creativity, strength, vitality, protective amulet, warrior stone, money, prosperity, courage, stamina, higher knowledge, purification, healing, body detox, divination, weather prediction. It is a sun-turning stone also called "heliotrope" because it turns red when it gets wet.

Carnelian   Activates kundalini energy, virility, protects against anger and fear and falling, motivation, creativity, past-life awareness, purification, releases sorrow, courage, strength, attracts fire elementals and winged dragons.

Citrine   Confidence, mental power, vitality, security, motivation, dispels negativity, strengthens self-esteem, helps manifest magical goals, prosperity, abundance, empowerment, shapeshifting.

Clear Quartz   Healing, divination, meditation, shapeshifting, power animals, out-of-body experience, second sight, purification, protection, balance.

Diamond   Amplifies your energy field, hardest substance of nature used for healing, strength, power, good fortune, sexuality, love, insight, inspiration, protection, personal development, multidimensional awareness.

Garnet   Prosperity, strength, love, passion, imagination, flow, friendship, creativity, past-life experience, good luck, cultivating compassion, calming anger, friendship, faith, protection, virility, trust.

Hematite   Grounding, centering, confidence, enhances circulation of body fluids, protection, strength, boosts self-esteem, harmony, calms nerves.

Herkimer Diamond   Dream magic, higher love, psychic development, dispels negativity, past-life experience, empowerment, reduces stress.

Mica   Mental clarity, focus, concentration, insight, public speaking, knowledge, communication skills.

Obsidian   Grounding, centering, dispels negativity, protection, working with your shadow self, courage, self-control, divination, ancestral communication, letting go of outdated behaviors and memories, past-life experience, forgiveness, sharpens insight.

Onyx   Story-telling stone, creates structure, balance, reduces stress, strength, soothes nerves, ancestral communication, getting in touch with your shadow self.

Pyrite   Good fortune, money, wealth, prosperity, business success, mental clarity, insight, concentration, focus, divination.

Red Jasper   Endurance, purification, fortitude, prayer, protection, mental agility, clarity, reduces stress.

Red Tourmaline   Balance; harmony; energizing body, mind, and spirit; balancing male and female energies; clarity; problem solving.

Ruby   Activates and amplifies your energy field, manifesting stone, creativity, strength, motivation, ambition, shapeshifting, timeshifting, insight, out-of-body experience, past-life experience, protection, love magic, friendship, noble purpose, attracts faeries.

Rutilated Quartz   Healing, directing energy, balance, second sight, magic power booster, wellness, dispels negativity, enhances sexuality and self-esteem.

Smoky Quartz   Grounding, centering, healing, dispels negativity, neutralizes energies, divination, insight, ancestral communication, protection.

Tiger's Eye   Balance, strength, insight, confidence, protection, focus, attaining goals, wealth, success, shapeshifting.

Topaz (golden)   Strengthens magic intention, loyalty, love magic, creativity, balance, healing, problem solving, reduces stress, expands second sight, attracts faeries.

Zircon (clear)   Look-alike diamond for harmony, balance, reserve, reflection, mirroring in magic, tolerance, patience, self-control.

WATER

Colors: Blue, sea green, purple, aqua, blue-green, gray, indigo, white, lavender, and pink stones

Amethyst   Faith, self-control, recommended for men to use for attracting women, divination, protection, healing, love magic, dream magic, banishes nightmares, mental clarity, courage, compassion, higher consciousness, psychic development, shapeshifting.

Aquamarine   Mental clarity, insight, inspiration, peace, harmony, good luck, flow, protection, increases intuition, calms stomach, dieting stone, out-of-body experience, soothes, reduces fears, attracts water faeries.

Azurite   Spirit guides, promotes communication, amplifies energy field, healing, heightens spiritual consciousness, clarity, meditation, divination, precognition, revitalizes the mind, promotes prenatal strength.

Blue Lace Agate   Joy, harmony, peace, happiness, good cheer, good luck, soothes emotions, mental clarity, attunes the body, mind, and spirit.

Calcite   Healing, mental clarity, concentration, focus, boosts memory, meditation, out-of-body experience, calms nerves.

Chrysocolla   Activates the divine feminine, sacred communication, balances emotions, confidence, musical ability, alleviates guilt, stress, and tension.

Clear Quartz   Healing, flow, divination, meditation, shapeshifting, past-life experience, second sight, psychic development, purification, protection, balance.

Coral   Woman's stone, protection, good luck, love magic, ancestral communication, moon magic, healing, fertility.

Jade   Love magic, protection, abundance, prosperity, calms, soothes nerves, dispels negativity, provides higher consciousness, purification, brings harmony, attracts nature spirits and spirit guides.

Labradorite   Elevates consciousness, psychic development, enhances protection, shapeshifting, and enhances divine communication.

Lapis Lazuli   Psychic development, divination, protection, self-knowledge, wisdom, courage, creativity, magical power, prosperity, out-of-body experience, shapeshifting, amplifies thoughts, calms nerves, boosts immune system, expands awareness, attracts nature spirits.

Lepidolite   Peace, harmony, good luck, dream magic, acceptance, out-of-body experience, increases psychic ability, soothes anger.

Lodestone   Love magic, fidelity, business success, prosperity, riches, protection, good luck, friendship, joy, hope.

Milky Quartz   Quartz with lunar powers, meditation, dream magic, faery magic, psychic development, past-life experience, ancestral communication.

Moonstone   Lunar power, feminine power, beauty, diet stone, receptivity, flow, cycles, out-of-body experience, scrying, balancing emotions, healing, enhancing sensitivity, intuition, clairvoyance, divination, artistic pursuits, good luck, fruitfulness, love magic.

Rose Quartz   Balances emotions, friendship, romance, love magic, compassion, attunement, forgiveness, self-acceptance, adapts to changes, heals, inner voice, faith, fertility, creativity, boosts self-esteem, attracts helpful faeries.

Sapphire   Psychic development, focus, creativity, calms emotions, harmony, balance, dispels negativity, out-of-body experience, healing, eases stress, concentration, meditation, divination, good fortune, stimulates energy centers, attracts faeries.

Sodalite   Mental clarity, agility, boosts the immune system, clairvoyance, balance, harmony, healing, stabilizing, neutralizes harmful energies.

Sugilite   Dream magic, divination, out-of-body experience, psychic development, past-life experience, energy amplifier.

WITCH AND WIZARD
TREES, FLOWERS, HERBS,
AND OILS

Alder Tree Protection, divination, out-of-body experience, dream magic, shapeshifting, wand tree, past-life experience, faery tree.

Almond Wealth, success, prosperity, abundance, love, expands awareness.

Aloe Healing, balance, harmony, rejuvenation, eases pain, relieves skin infections, burns, sunburn, poison oak or poison ivy.

Apple Longevity, immortality, vitality, magic wand tree, healing, love magic, fertility, friendship, abundance, image magic, happiness, beauty, joy, hope, attracts faeries.

Apricot Love, friendship, beauty, good cheer, magic wand tree, creativity, mental clarity, focus, expands awareness.

Ash Communication, knowledge, magic wand tree, healing, sacred union of the divine feminine and masculine, creativity, rebirth, prophecy, justice.

Barley Prosperity, wealth, abundance, dispels negativity, soothes body, harmony.

Basil (sweet) Uplifts mind, creativity, love magic, fertility, sexuality, protection, good luck, success, empowerment.

Bay Laurel Divination, dream magic, protection, magic power, psychic development, alters states of awareness, endurance, healing, increases intuition, magic wand tree, purification, attracts nature spirits, shapeshifting.

Bee Pollen   Endurance, strength, healing, increases memory, rejuvenates, renews, restores.

Beech   Ancestral communication, past-life experience, prosperity, inheritance, magic wand tree, second sight.

Bergamot   Love magic, harmony, peace, dream magic, reduces stress, uplifts body, mind, and spirit, and healing. (*Note:* Bergamot makes your skin UV light sensitive, so avoid prolonged sun exposure for up to twelve hours after using it.)

Birch   New beginnings, rebirth, structure, protection, formation, regeneration, renewal, magic wand tree.

Blackberry   Protection, healing, prosperity, abundance, attracts faeries.

Blessed Thistle   Mental clarity and agility, purification, cleansing, divination, wellness, heals, dispels negativity, strengthens memory.

Bluebells   Joy, peace, happiness, merriment, attracts flower faeries.

Burdock   Purification, cleansing, protection, harmony, dispels negativity, balance.

Carnation   Healing, blessings, joy, hope, good health, protection, attracts winged faeries.

Catnip   Harmony, peace, love magic, friendship, happiness, joy, playfulness, healing, wellness, beauty, dream magic, calms your nerves, balances emotions. Cats love it!

Cayenne   Catalyst for all herbs, increases circulation, purifies your blood, healing tonic, calms nerves, wellness, relaxation (*Note:* Handle with care, as it can be irritating to your mucous membranes and may cause a burning sensation.)

Cedarwood   Harmony, peace, wellness, healing, soothes nerves, magic wand tree, purification, protection, prosperity, wealth, wisdom, and herb of the sun. (*Note*: Do not use this oil on infants or small children. Always first dilute with a carrier oil, as pure cedarwood is very irritating to the skin. Use a maximum of two or three drops of cedarwood essential oil in bathwater.)

Chamomile   Love magic, friendship, harmony, wellness, healing, prosperity, abundance, money, purification, meditation, protection, dispels negative energy, attracts flower faeries, reduces stress, boosts immune system.

Cherry   Love magic, enhances sexuality, joy, playfulness, beauty, happiness, enhances sensuality, divination, magic wand tree.

Clover   Relaxes, vitalizes, healing, calms nerves, dispels negativity, love magic, harmony, peace, fertility, good luck, good fortune, money, prophecy, mental clarity, out-of-body experience, attracts helpful nature spirits.

Coriander   Love magic, sexuality, virility, prowess, rejuvenation.

Daisy   A faery favorite, peace, harmony, merriment, playfulness, love magic, enhances sensuality, solves problems.

Damiana   Renewal, rejuvenation, sexuality, passion, love magic, attracts love.

Dandelion   Psychic development, healing, wellness, balance, harmony, hope, wishes, vitality, enhances intuition, attracts winged faeries.

Dogwood   Beauty, hope, beginnings, protection, enchantment, four-petaled flowers attract helpful earth, air, fire, and water faeries, magic wand tree.

Dragon's Blood   Love magic, prowess, protection, dispels negativity, increases magic power.

Echinacea   Healing, wellness, natural antibiotic, boosts immune system, increases magic power.

Elder   Magic wand tree, protection, blessing, prosperity, creativity, increases magic power.

Eyebright   Mental clarity, focus, intuition, insight, psychic development, clairvoyance.

Fennel   Healing, wellness, purification, harmony, tranquility, longevity, courage, vigor, protection, soothes stomach. (Use only in small amounts.)

Flax   Healing, wellness, protection, dispels negativity, divination.

Frankincense   Divination, protection, purification, cleansing, meditation, psychic development, shapeshifting, out-of-body experience, balance, harmony, calms nerves, helps in merging.

Garlic   Healing, wellness, rejuvenation, body detox, dispels negativity, prosperity, wealth, success, good fortune, protective amulet, acts as an energy shield.

Geranium   Healing, wellness, harmony, abundance, enrichment.

Ginger   Empowerment, love magic, strengthens body, mind, and spirit, harmony, peace, tranquility, balance.

Ginkgo Biloba   Healing, wellness, psychic development, intuition, mental clarity, focus, concentration, memory, reaction time, longevity.

Ginseng (American)   Increases strength, vigor, focus, concentration, promotes mental activities, stimulates body, reduces tension and fatigue, nourishes blood, enhances creativity, attracts positive energies, beauty, harmony, peace of mind. (*Note*: People with high blood pressure should not use ginseng in any form.)

Ginseng (wild Siberian)   Love magic, sex magic, restores sexual centers, healing, wishes, beauty, protection, longevity. (*Note*: People with high blood pressure should not use ginseng in any form.)

Golden Seal   Healing, purification, cleansing, natural antibiotic, raises metabolism and body temperature.

Gotu Kola   Longevity, rejuvenation, regeneration, calms nerves, mental clarity, focus, concentration, helps in learning, divination, memory retention, meditation.

Hawthorn   Shapeshifting, prosperity, inheritance, sacred union of the divine feminine and masculine, love magic, fertility, magic wand tree.

Hazel   Fertility, wisdom, knowledge, protection, magic wand tree, insight, divination, dowsing, healing, purification, meditation.

Heather   Attracts faeries, love magic, expands awareness, psychic development.

Holly   Ancestral communication, divination, concentration, organization, intelligence, sacred union of the divine feminine and masculine, rebirth.

Hollyhock   Abundance, wealth, riches, prosperity, attracts flower faeries, increases magic power, healing, good luck, second sight.

Honeysuckle   Love magic, sexuality, passion, prowess, out-of-body experience, attracts nature spirits, helps in merging, dream magic, protection, beauty, hope, attracts positive relationships.

Horny Goat Weed   Sexuality, stimulates male energy, love magic.

Iris   A flower of wisdom and faith as well as eternal beauty. Plant irises in your garden to attract noble and helpful faeries, especially faery queens and kings.

Jasmine   Love magic, dream magic, attracts nature spirits, prosperity, magic power, hope, romance, compassion, sexuality, divination, creativity, attracts lovers.

Lavender   Healing, peace, joy, hope, harmony, tranquility, dream magic, divination, out-of-body experience, expands awareness, protection, love magic, purification, attracts men, attracts nature spirits, repels insects, dispels negativity. Sprinkle a few drops of the essential oil on bed linens for sweet dreams.

Lemon   Cleansing, healing, purification, joy, harmony, reduces stress, calms nerves, friendship, insight.

Licorice Root   Love magic, sexuality, vigor, fidelity, vitality.

Lilac   Love magic, peace, harmony, romance, protection, boosts memory, attracts flower faeries.

Marigold   Lucid dreaming, psychic development, intuition, clairvoyant dreams, shapeshifting, timeshifting, protection, second sight, enhances magic power, attracts helpful faeries.

Marjoram   Love magic, fertility, marriage/handfasting, desire, passion, joy, harmony, peace, vitality, dispels negativity, healing, uplifts emotions, protection, balance, wellness. (*Note:* Too much marjoram can stupefy. Do not use marjoram oil if you have low blood pressure, suffer from depression, or are pregnant.)

Marshmallow Herb   Healing, wellness, good health, calms nerves, dispels negativity, psychic development, divination, purification, spirit magnet.

Meadowsweet   Love magic, passion, romance, desire, sexuality, fertility, marriage/handfasting, uplifts emotions, joy, hope, beauty, enhances magic power, attracts nature spirits.

Milkweed   Wishes, hope, joy, prophecy, dream magic, expands awareness, attracts butterflies and faeries.

Mint   Protection, dispels negativity, focus, concentration, mental clarity, healing, wellness, soothes body, dream magic, travel amulet, increases memory, learning, attracts winged faeries.

Mistletoe   Beauty, love magic, desire, protection, enhances magic power, dispels negativity, healing, dream magic, bird augury, prophecy, divination, attracts nature spirits. (*Note*: Do not ingest mistletoe berries, wood, or leaves.)

Mugwort   Prophecy, dream magic, protection, psychic development, out-of-body experience, divination, enhances magic power.

Myrrh   Healing, wellness, protection, strength, courage, vitality, increases energy, stamina, endurance, harmony, balance, merging.

Neroli   harmony, joy, hope, love, romance, balances emotions, sweetens life, releases grief, reduces stress, calms nerves, attracts nature spirits.

Nettle   Healing, soothes skin, calms nerves, purification, cleansing, protection.

Oak   Powerful tree magic, ancestral communication, justice, loyalty, victory, success, prosperity, wealth, endurance, strength, fertility, vision, protection, regeneration, a place where nature spirits reside, magic wand tree.

Pansy   Love magic, desire, passion, romance, sexuality, playfulness, attracts faeries.

Passion Flower   Harmony, peace, happiness, joy, calms your mind, protection, passion, desire, love magic, merging, expands awareness, creativity, dream magic.

Patchouli   Love magic, romance, desire, passion, sexuality, psychic development, mental clarity, clairvoyance, shapeshifting, uplifts emotions, healing, wellness, attracts lovers.

Peach   Magic wand tree, friendship, love, good luck, fruitfulness, passion, desire, romance, merriment, playfulness, joy, hope.

Pear   Magic wand tree, joy, hope, happiness, sacred union of the divine feminine and masculine, prosperity, fruitfulness, completion.

Pine   Magic wand tree, healing, wellness, reduces fatigue, creativity, mental clarity, abundance, prosperity, wealth, protection, purification, regeneration, love magic, friendship, romance, fertility, dispels negativity, integrates body, mind, and spirit.

Rose   Love magic, desire, romance, passion, sexuality, stimulates senses, compassion, balances female and male energies, abundance, good fortune, prosperity, wealth, riches, divination, healing, good health, dream magic, enhances magic power, protection, peace of mind, harmony, joy, good luck, attracts faeries. Fossils of roses exist that were grown more than 32 million years ago.

Rosemary (Elf Leaf)   Love magic, desire, passion, mental clarity, focus, learning, strength, courage, healing, wellness, vitality, vigor, stimulates mind, memory booster, problem solving, dispels negativity, protection, purification, expands awareness, attracts helpful elves.

Rowan   Magic wand tree, protection, healing, wellness, attracts helpful faeries.

Saffron   Dream magic, love magic, healing, second sight, purification, prophecy, merging, enhances magic power, weather magic.

Sage   Cleansing, purification, healing, wellness, longevity, focus, concentration, mental clarity, wisdom, protection, vitality, learning, increases memory, dispels negativity, reduces stress, meditation, dream protection. (*Note*: Stimulating in small doses, but sedating and toxic in large doses.)

St. John's Wort   Healing, wellness, purification, blessing, attracts helpful nature spirits.

Sandalwood   Protection, purification, love magic, sex magic, relaxation, harmony, joy, shapeshifting, healing, expands awareness, calms nerves, increases magic power.

Skullcap   Calms and strengthens nerves, harmony, peace of mind, balances emotions, higher love, relaxation.

Spruce   Magic wand tree, psychic development, enlightenment, intuition, wellness, spiritual awakening.

Sunflowers   Prosperity, wealth, abundance, riches, fertility, strength, visions, love magic, attracts flower faeries.

Thyme   Expands awareness, healing, purification, enhances magic power, second sight, opening to love, letting go of outdated behaviors and memories, attracts garden faeries.

Valerian Root   Healing, wellness, promotes sound sleep, expands awareness, dispels negativity, spirit world communication, strengthens magic power, cat magic.

Vanilla   Love magic, sexuality, romance, desire, passion, lust, harmony, relaxation, mental agility, playfulness.

Vervain   Love magic, purification, starwalking, initiation, dream magic, grace, divination, healing, dispels negativity, protection, prophetic dreams.

Violet   Love magic, desire, passion, lust, sexuality, second sight, dream magic, attracts flower faeries.

White Poplar (Aspen)   Protection, prevents illness, rebirth, ancestral communication, peace, harmony, balance, magic wand tree.

Wild Yam Root   Balances feminine sexual energies, soothes body, relaxation, harmony.

Willow   Powerful tree magic, healing, fertility, enchantment, shapeshifting, ancestral communication, visions, birth, attracts water spirits, magic wand tree.

Yew   Magic wand tree, rebirth, adaptability, flexibility, strength, ancestral communication, transformation, change, protection, regeneration, dream magic, divination, longevity.

Ylang-ylang   Love magic, romance, desire, passion, lust, sexuality, harmony, fertility, relaxation, healing, regulates adrenaline, encourages hair growth.

Yohimbe   Activates sexuality, love magic, desire, passion, lust, stimulates the body.

WITCH AND WIZARD RUNES

The ancient rune symbols are living symbols as they represent dynamic changing and evolving forces. Inscribed on talismans, on charms, on rune rings, and on candles, runes are both powerful and easy to use. During meditation and practicing magic, runelike symbols of light can be seen on the insides of your eyes when you close them. These patterns, called phosphenes, originate in your brain's visual cortex and neural system. The following lists the Elder Futhark runes:

Name: Fehu, pronounced: fay-hoo
Sound: F
Divination meaning: Wealth and abundance in accordance with the primal forces of creation.

Name: Uruz, pronounced: ooo-ruse
Sound: U
Divination meaning: Static structure, giving form and structure to the primal creativity.

Name: Thurisaz, pronounced: thur-ee-saws
Sound: the unvoiced "th" as in thorn
Divination meaning: Protection, a thorny vine that provides defense against invaders.

Name: Ansuz, pronounced: awn-sooz
Sound: AA (ah)
Divination meaning: Divine knowledge, wisdom, rebirth, creative expression.

Name: Raidho, pronounced: rye-tho
Sound: R
Divination meaning: Represents the solar wagon, circular flow, rhythm, travel.

Name: Kenaz, pronounced: kane-awz
Sound: K
Divination meaning: Knowledge, the internal fire, the guiding light.

Name: Gebo, pronounced: gay-bow
Sound: G
Divination meaning: The Divine gift, exchange, interaction, balance.

Name: Wunjo, pronounced: woon-yo
Sound: W
Divination meaning: Joy, pleasure, hope, kinship, fellowship, wonderment.

Name: Hagalaz, pronounced: haw-ga-laws
Sound: H
Divination meaning: Associated with the Norn Urd, the past, transformation, evolution, merging, harmony, protection.

Name: Naudhiz, pronounced now-these
Sound: N
Divination meaning: Associated with the Norn Verdandi, the need fire, help, resistance, passion, love, shadow self.

Name: Isa, pronounced: ee-saw
Sound: short I
Divination meaning: Associated with the Norn Skuld, ice, slow-moving structure, stasis, delay, gradual integration.

Name: Jera, pronounced: yar-awe
Sound: Y
Divination meaning: Signifies the life cycle and cycle of the Sun, completion, fertility, natural law, progression.

Name: Eihwaz, pronounced: eye-waz
Sound: E and long I
Divination meaning: Symbolic of the yew tree, transcendence, death, rebirth, communication, knowledge, dreaming, magic.

Name: Perthro, pronounced: perth-row
Sound: P
Divination meaning: The turning over of the dice cup, chance, birth, wisdom, luck.

Name: Algiz, pronounced: all-geez
Sound: Z
Divination meaning: A protective force, spirit, sanctuary, refuge, power, divinity.

Name: Sowilo, pronounced: so-wheel-o
Sound: S
Divination meaning: The Divine solar wheel, partnership, power, transformation, understanding.

Name: Tiwaz, pronounced: tea-waz
Sound: T
Divination meaning: Justice, order, victory, loyalty, the mystery of spirituality and faith.

Name: Berkana, pronounced: bur-kan-a
Sound: B
Divination meaning: The Birch goddess, nurturing, rebirth, growth, spirit, concealment, ancestry, transition.

Name: Ehwaz, pronounced: ee-waz
Sound: E
Divination meaning: Duality, twins, nature, movement, partnership, interaction, harmony, traveling to other dimensions.

Name: Mannaz, pronounced: man-nawz
Sound: M
Divination meaning: Represents the "rainbow bridge," moving from this world to the world of the Divine, memory, human, order, intelligence, ancestors, sacred union.

Name: Laguz, pronounced: la-gooz
Sound: L
Divination meaning: Embodies the element of Water, fluidity, life force, birth.

Name: Ingwaz, pronounced: ing-waz
Sound: I
Divination meaning: Embodies the element of Earth, fertility, the seed, energy, gestation, integration.

Name: Dagaz, pronounced: thay-gaz
Sound: hard th
Divination meaning: Embodies the element of Fire, enlightenment, polarity, intuition, well-being, knowledge of the powers of light and dark.

Name: Othala, pronounced: oath-awe-la
Sound: O
Divination meaning: Embodies the element of Air, ancestral connections, prosperity, property, Oneness.

ALPHABETICAL CORRESPONDENCES
TO THE RUNES

A—Ansuz

B—Berkana

C—Kenaz

D—Dagaz

E—Ehwaz

F—Fehu

G—Gebo

H—Hagalaz

I—Isa or Eihwaz

J—Jera or Isa

K—Kenaz

L—Laguz

M—Mannaz

N—Naudhiz

NG—Ingwaz

O—Othala

P—Perdhro

Q—Kenaz

R—Raidho

S—Sowilo

T—Tiwaz

TH—Thurisaz and Dagaz

U—Uruz

V—Wunjo or Uruz

W—Wunjo

X—Kenaz plus Sowilo

Y—Jera

Z—Algiz or Sowilo

Final E, Z, or R—Algiz

APPENDIX D

WITCH AND WIZARD
SHAPESHIFTING BESTIARY

*A word to the wise is to work with only positive, helpful animals and magical creatures when shapeshifting.

Aardvark Longevity of life and relationships, good health, and prolonging experiences. If an aardvark crosses your path, you will live to be a hundred years old.

Abraxen Developing your power, strength, service, potential, loyalty, endurance. An abraxen is an elephant-sized flying palomino horse.

Acromantula Balancing offensive and defensive power, violence, death, wisdom, longevity. The acromantula is a giant spider.

Alligator Integrating experiences and lessons, throwing enemies off balance, changing directions, flexibility. The alligator is sacred to Native American tribes on the East Coast of the United States.

Anaconda Precognition, divination, clairvoyance, telepathy, lucid dreaming, foresight, future telling. The anaconda is the largest snake in the world and is considered a teacher animal in the Amazon.

Ant Learning to be here now, in the moment, developing personal patience, humility, working in your community, planning, setting realistic goals.

Anteater Ability to smell trouble before walking into it, developing skills for finding lost objects and people, and finding solutions.

Antelope Creating patterns, taking quick and immediate action, active force and drive, enthusiasm, inspiration, and swiftness, teaching you to do it now and not to procrastinate.

Armadillo   Giving protection, setting up personal boundaries, discrimination, respecting the sacred space of others, and shielding from negative energies.

Baboon   Listening to divine messages, heeding warnings, defending your family, creating natural order and patterns, and finding lost people and objects. The Egyptians trained the baboon to stack firewood. Thoth is portrayed as a baboon standing in the Judgment Hall of Osiris in the land of the dead.

Badger   Taking charge, force and power, acting in times of emergency, overcoming fears, self-expression, trusting your inherent abilities, attunement with the Earth, protection, and dealing with difficult and dangerous situations and people.

Basilisk   Fierce power, longevity, transformation, death, and violence. The basilisk is extremely poisonous, and its breath, touch, and look are fatal. It often appears with a spotted crest, like the cobra, denoting kingship among the serpents. The crowing of a rooster kills the basilisk.

Bat   Shapeshifting, transformation, overturning habits and enemies, experiencing new adventures and revealing potential, ability to use sound vibration as a means of communication, transitions, tapping into past lives, and meeting new people.

Bear   Courage, healing ability, dream magic, protection, fury, survival, endurance, stamina, crystal magic, herb magic, finding personal options, building inner strengths and knowing, tapping into the magnetic currents within the Earth, connection with the Goddess, introspection, ability to spend long periods in solitude, and strength in the face of adversity.

Beaver   Industriousness, responsibility, constructing patterns, building shelter, buying land and real estate, developing skills and knowledge, envisioning your dreams, crafting with your hands, natural harmony, making plans, and protection.

Bee   Accomplishing tasks, learning to be more productive, following through, working in harmony with nature, feminine potency, communication skills, teamwork, messenger of the Goddess, reincarnation, cooperative efforts, and working toward the common good. Without bees there would be no flowers and fruits.

Beetle Renewal and regeneration, restoration of power and energy, rebirth, reincarnation, past-life experience, and ancestral communication.

Bighorn Sheep Meeting goals through self-effort, developing skills, endurance, climbing out of difficulties, meeting negativity head-on, and succeeding in business ventures.

Blackbird Developing your magical abilities, doing trance work, using camouflage for protection, and flexibility. Druid Dubh means "The druid bird." Druid Dubh is the first of the Oldest Animals.

Bluebird Creating body, mind, and spirit happiness, active mind, joy, positive mental thought, modesty, and divine inspiration.

Blue Jay Learning to be a master of disguise, mimicking ability, warning of present dangers, seeing through masks, getting in touch with your power voice, flexibility, bold action, heeding warnings, spotting trouble and potential problems, positive disruption, communication, agility, and adaptability.

Boa Constrictor Flexibility, timely moment, decision making, timing goals and patterns, expanding horizons, and physical agility of the body.

Boar Courage, confrontation, bravery in combat, meeting risk and danger head-on, determination, and regaining wild power. The boar is a power animal of the Mayan hunters.

Boarhound Protection, courage, instinctual action, and loyalty. Fang is a boarhound.

Bobcat Looking at a situation from the outside in, developing your skills of watching and waiting for the right time, seeing in dark places, and vigilance.

Boggart Mischief, practical jokes, pranks, danger, enemies near, shapeshifting, transformation, change, supernatural ability, and a dark creature. The boggart is a hobgoblin or ghost that fears automobiles and bears. Boggarts can attach themselves to families, and are difficult to get rid of. They will not come out when the moon is bright.

Buffalo Communicating with ancestors, creating abundance and prosperity, well-being, magic power, spiritual inspiration, manifesting goals, getting around barriers, good health, learning to be receptive, and becoming a leader.

Bull Breaking through barriers in your profession or personal relationships, increasing sexuality and fertility, developing personal power and strength in difficult times, and working toward a single goal. Zeus took the form of a bull to seduce women.

Butterfly Developing your self-esteem, transformation, metamorphosis, transmigration, embracing your visions and dreams, freedom, expressing your soul energy, and understanding your innate beauty.

Camel Building endurance, gathering resources together and using them wisely, transforming burden, regulating energy, budgeting finances, unpredictable behavior, finding your way, and being prepared.

Cardinal (Redbird) Learning skills of parenthood, especially fatherhood, honing courtship abilities and power of attraction, developing your singing ability, and discovering your inner song.

Caribou/Reindeer Physical strength, athletic ability, balancing body, mind, and spirit, body knowledge, social skills, traveling at night, protection for travelers, homing abilities, and playing fair.

Cat Developing a sense of independence, learning to love yourself, sensuality and sensory ability, extrasensory and magical powers, developing poise and agility, transformation, meditation, seeing the unseen, cleverness, stealth, cunning, playfulness, keeping secrets, and dimensional companionship. Cats make excellent witch and wizard familiars.

Caterpillar Transformation, using every resource at hand, going slowly from a to b to c in professional goals, welcoming slow and natural personal change, and shedding past grievances and doubts.

Centipede Cooperative and coordinated action, working in unity with others, integrating body, mind, and spirit, and focusing on one goal at a time.

Centaur Protection, shapeshifting, supernatural ability, quickness, strength, power, mystery, powers of observation and divination. Associated with the constellation Sagittarius, Centaurs are a forest and mountain race of monsters that lived in Thessaly in Greek mythology that were half horse and half man.

Chameleon Adapting to change, shifting perception and views, blending with environment, external harmony, and working in tandem with others.

Cheetah Precise movement, swiftness, blending with your surroundings, accomplishing many goals at once and suddenly, orchestrating large patterns, developing organizational skills, and developing personal insight and your powers of observation.

Chimera Violence, cold-blooded action, death, destruction, tragedy. In Greek mythology, a monster with the head of a lion, body of a goat, and tail of a serpent that breathes fire and destroys everything in its wake with flame.

Chimpanzee Bonding in relationships, learning how to touch others in positive ways, helping others, and working in groups cooperatively.

Chipmunk Respect for children and animals, tending to the small details of daily life, gathering resources, and being resourceful.

Cockatrice Danger, sign of death and destruction, tragedy, violence, pain, horror. Appears with the head of a cock, the wings and feet of a fowl, and a barbed serpent's tail.

Cockroach Understanding your shadow self, facing fear, surviving, sudden and quick movement, cunning, being persistent, and developing your abilities of concealment.

Cock/Rooster Teaching you how to evoke the attention and desires of others, gathering sexual energy, and developing personal ambition.

Clam   Keeping secrets, autonomous action, self-containment and maintenance, inner knowledge, and protection.

Cobra   Accessing the ancient wisdom, kundalini awakening, invisible powers, force, grasping ideas, psychic vision, divination, aggressive action, transformation. The cobra is a talisman of the ancient mystery traditions. Cobra is the awakener.

Cockatoo   Forgiving, healing self-hatred, and letting go of old patterns

Cougar (Mountain Lion)   Developing inner courage and bravery, learning how to push the envelope, chasing suddenly and swiftly, and developing self-responsibility.

Cow   Learning acceptance, recognizing natural harmony in all things, and appreciating others. In Celtic tradition, white cow's milk is said to have healing properties. In Ireland, three magical cows, one white, one red, and one black in color, arose from the sea.

Coyote   Working with your shadow self, playing practical jokes, unmasking hidden desires, shapeshifting, trickery, and witticisms, developing a mischievous sense of humor, demonstrating independence, using laughter as therapy, using deception for protection, and balancing risk with safety. The coyote's time is the gap between day and night.

Crab   Taking alternative action, turning patterns around, sidestepping trouble and problems, digging in and holding your ground, and learning caution.

Crane   Adding longevity to all your patterns, reincarnation, transmigration, communicating with and contacting ancestors, and increasing dancing ability, natural sexuality, and romantic appeal.

Cricket   Learning to use sound for healing the body, mind, and spirit, good luck, harmony, working in unison with nature, developing your voice and singing ability, speaking ability, and finding your personal song.

Crocodile   Manifesting patterns, working together with nature, attaining your goals, transformation, and change. The Aborigines of

Australia feel the crocodile is the ancient spirit of the Earth Mother.

Crow   Ridding yourself of negativity, focusing on skills and positive talents, using disorder to your advantage, and taking the opportunities that are presented to you.

Cuckoo   Learning how to mimic the behavior of other animals and people, developing personal talents and skills, beginning new enterprises, giving divine inspiration and guidance, having fun, performing, and entertaining,

Deer   Developing compassion, sensitivity, grace, agility, kindness, gentleness, proceeding with caution, learning tenderness and gratitude, practicing ability to listen, smelling danger, being watchful, forest magic, and paying attention to natural signs and messages.

Dingo   Learning to follow through, protection, ability to locate lost people and things, providing companionship, and developing a sense of loyalty to yourself and to others.

Dinosaur   Learning how to use ancient wisdom, listening to the spirits of the sacred land, and orchestrating large projects.

Dog   Developing loyalty, both to yourself and to others, unconditional love, protection of patterns and possessions, friendship, companionship, heightened senses, tracking ability, intuition, developing instinctual awareness and personal integrity, and faithfulness. The dog is associated with healing as its saliva is said to have curative properties. Dogs make excellent witch and wizard familiars.

Dolphin   How to use energy wisely, finding joy, love, and playfulness in daily life, using your breathing to access altered states of consciousness, developing natural intelligence and grace, eloquence, heightened communication, knowledge of the sea, and dream magic. The dolphin is called the Hermes of the sea.

Donkey/Ass   Digging in, endurance, strength and humility, saying no to others, not being swayed by the opinions of others, and accepting duty.

Dove   Merging with oneness, learning to trust yourself and others, inner calm, experiencing peace, joy, and love, and positive movement toward the successful outcome of your patterns.

Doxy   Pestilence, danger, warning, harm, infestation of negativity. A doxy looks like a small biting faery covered with black hair. Doxies are poisonous.

Dragon (winged)   Conscious awareness, magical ability and skills, creative ability, altering your consciousness, communicating with ancestors, creating personal patterns, gathering resources, and awakening ancient memories.

Dragonfly   Moving beyond your present awareness, lifting the veils of perception, experiencing multidimensional travel, having lucid dreams, transmigration, and developing magical abilities.

Duck   Free will, positive emotion and action, prosperity, plenty, following your heart and inner feelings, and self-responsibility.

Eagle   Divine connection, nobility, discrimination, inspiration, courage, wisdom, and creative power, messages and gifts from the spirits, applied power and sheer will, making the best choices possible, unleashing your imagination, clear sight, keen powers of observation. Sacred to many cultures, the eagle is associated with the Sun. It flies higher and over greater distances and sees further than any other bird. The eagle is the highest expression of spirit.

Earthworm   Learning the natural balance of female and male aspects within yourself, digging in, and using the resources on hand.

Eel   Conductivity of energy such as love, passion, psychic impressions, and electrifying patterns.

Elephant   Manifesting goals, strength, prosperity, wisdom, happiness, removing obstacles, discovering answers, problem solving, and utilizing all educational opportunities. The Zulus of Africa say the elephant brings happiness, peace, and tranquility into the home. The elephant is the Lord of Solutions.

Elk   Teaches stamina, persistence, and endurance, developing concentration and focus, passion, and following through in personal and professional goals.

Emu Balancing your heart and head, using intuition and reasoning abilities together in harmony, and letting go of old behaviors and thoughts.

Falcon Swiftness, power, insight, developing psychic ability and alchemical mastery, learning to ask the correct questions, receiving divine guidance, and experiencing multidimensional awareness and travel.

Ferret Taking direct action, demonstrating ingenuity, cutting through red tape, developing cunning and craftiness, building physical energy, flexibility, solving mysteries and finding hidden secrets, self-discovery, and finding lost objects and people.

Finch Building desire, passion, love, new beginnings and adventures, making successful choices and decisions, showing enthusiasm, and gaining boundless energy.

Firefly (Lightning Bug) Providing enlightenment and illumination, enthusiasm, sharing energy wisely, developing skills in the performing arts, and employing the element of surprise.

Fish Staying in the flow, adapting to situations, and feeling renewal.

Flamingo Learning trust, open-heartedness, compassion, open-mindedness, beauty, loving nature, and accessing natural harmony.

Flea Quick and frequent change, swift movement, problem solving, endurance, adaptability, and alternative action.

Flicker Bird (Woodpecker) Used for protection, creates natural harmony and balance, heightened awareness, developing a sense of humor, learning to be cautious, and avoiding carelessness. In Native American traditions, the flicker bird's feather is used to keep negativity and harm at bay.

Fly Seeing with multifaceted vision, having a heightened sense of smell, using all materials on hand, and adapting to all environments and any kind of change. Noticing habits of animals and other people, eliminating personal vices, making conscious choices, and seeing the small details.

Fox Using the powers of camouflage, developing your powers of observation, hiding secrets, blending in with your environment, learning how to outwit those that would do you harm, and developing persistence and swiftness.

Frog Cleansing, purifying, letting go of old patterns, finding the transformative power of love, metamorphosis, developing new abilities such as a singing ability, releasing emotions, grief, and old habits, predicting the weather and bringing rain, new beginnings, and revitalizing your body.

Giraffe Finding new horizons, stretching your imagination and talents, discovering new experiences and adventures, reaching for the unattainable, and learning how to effectively pattern your life.

Goat Appreciation, friendship, and gratitude; endurance and survival; using limited resources; protection and defense; independence; surefootedness; agility; and adaptability.

Goose Imparting ancestral wisdom and knowledge, bringing abundance and plenty into your daily life, and providing protection.

Gorilla Communicating through action, and strengthening your intention and personal will, quiet strength, benevolence, and intelligent communication.

Grasshopper Learning how to tap into the natural cycles of the Earth, gathering and using resources wisely, collecting those things needed to succeed in life, showing respect for others and material wealth, appreciating divine gifts, making leaps of faith, overcoming obstacles, and welcoming quick and sudden change.

Griffin Providing protection of gold, riches, and treasure, guarding finances, powerful ally in business, justice, honor, respect, and royal purpose. Griffins appear with eagles' heads and wings, lions' bodies, and serpents' tails. They pull the chariot of the Sun and dislike horses immensely.

Hamster (Guinea Pig) Being adaptable, getting rid of old beliefs and habits, using resources wisely, and working out the small details in life.

Hare (Rabbit) Being fertile and giving birth, bringing good luck, acting fearless and quick, learning how to listen to your inner voice, hiding secrets, conceiving ideas, living by your wits, and agility. The rabbit's foot is carried for fertility.

Hawk   Giving us clarity, vision, illumination, spirit messenger, divination, foretelling and insight, teaching us to listen to and understand nature, developing stamina, magic power, and noble awareness.

Hedgehog   Learning how to stay centered and grounded in the midst of chaos, minding your own business and keeping others out of your business, understanding weather patterns, being fertile, and learning how to direct your awareness.

Hen   Nurturing energies and following through, taking the appropriate steps toward personal goals, discerning the pecking order, and doing community work.

Heron   Introspection, intuition, self-improvement, self-responsibility, exploring new ideas, and self-reliance.

Hippocampus   Supernatural power, danger, warning, caution. A hippocampus draws Poseidon's chariot and appears with the head and body of a horse with a large fishlike sea monster hind end. Babies are called tadfoals.

Hippogriff   A sense of freedom and supernatural ability, sudden and positive change, loyalty, service, and protection from enemies. Appears as horse-sized flying eagle with orange eyes. If you meet one, maintain eye contact and bow, until the animal bows back.

Hippopotamus   Appropriate use of aggression and fury, birthing of new ideas and associations, physical strength, protection, and ability to act alone when necessary.

Hornet   Learning the proper use of anger and fury to defend yourself if necessary, and providing constructive change of lifestyle.

Horse   Learning how to use power correctly, receiving divine inspiration and creativity; taking authoritative action and standing tall; warning of possible danger; and developing inner awareness and quickness of thought. Magical steeds abound in Celtic mythology, and among the Celtic people, there were few animals more loved than the horse. As a power animal, the horse can carry you fast and far through otherworlds.

Hummingbird   Taking joy in life, finding romantic love and intimacy, seeing the positive aspects in daily life, receiving divine messages, feeling natural healing energy, and opening yourself up to the Earthly delights and pleasures.

Ibis   Tapping into ancient wisdom, developing your magical abilities, enlightenment, teaching, humor, alchemy, and universal knowledge. The ibis was sacred to the Egyptian goddess Isis. Thoth, god of the Moon and wisdom, has an ibis's head. Thoth, in the form of Ibis, hovered above the Egyptians and taught them the occult arts and sciences.

Iguana   Developing your sexuality and healthy sexual attitudes, learning positive intimacy, and experiencing sacred love.

Jackal   Experiencing astral travel and having out-of-body experiences, ability to see in the dark, accessing past lives and future lives, and kinship with the constellation of Orion and Egyptian mythology.

Jaguar   Developing personal integrity and spiritual balance, learning leadership skills, and using power wisely and mindfully.

Kangaroo   Protecting children, balancing evil, creating foundations for future generations, leaping away from trouble, possessing the ability to adapt to new situations, abundance, and prosperity.

Kingfisher   Gaining peace, happiness, and love; having clear and insightful vision; and dealing with your emotions, and dreaming.

Koala   Learning thoughtfulness and consideration, taking enough time to complete your projects successfully, climbing above obstacles, performing disciplines associated with slow yoga movements.

Ladybug   Unexpected gifts, sheer delight, learning how to give and receive, gaining natural balance, receiving spiritual enlightenment, and death and rebirth.

Leopard   Honoring your choices, avoiding danger, heeding warnings, confronting your fear and enemies, clarity, sharp mind, divine inspiration, making wise choices, ease of decision, stalking your opponent, and using power in positive ways.

Lion   Strength, personal prowess, self-assuredness, courage, cunning, watchfulness, fierce power, working cooperatively, ability to relax, and working together as a family.

Lizard Accessing your dreams with dream magic and having lucid dreams, learning how to use dreams for healing and out-of-body travel, venturing into the unknown, using powers of regeneration, facing fears, and expanding your vision.

Llama Developing your imagination, dreaming, and using divination for creativity and inspiration, and being playful.

Loon Enhancing your inner knowing, developing inner voice(s), using your voice to direct energy, psychic ability, astral travel, and intuition.

Lynx Learning how to trust and confide in others, keeping secrets, maintaining quiet wisdom, and developing your "watcher" skills.

Magpie Becoming a guardian of nature, preserving natural resources, and developing a connection with nature. The Pautes call the magpie the little black buffalo.

Manatee Learning gentleness, connecting with your true emotions and feelings, and living your life without leaving traces.

Manta Ray Teaching how to be a friend and how to trust, and escaping conflict and negativity.

Meerkat Nurturing feminine qualities, learning to live in a community, working toward the common good, caretaking the land, and developing your powers of observation.

Mermaid/Merman Magical water creatures with fish tails and webbed fingers, either female (mermaid) or male (merman), that live in airy places beneath the waves. Awakening the ancient mysteries, using ancestral power, learning how to flow, expressing your emotions and sexuality, and exploring new frontiers.

Mockingbird Learning through experience, changing your attitudes, overcoming fears and phobias, protecting your territory, developing intelligence, and taking advantage of educational opportunities.

Mole Finding hidden things and lost children, increasing foresight, developing your sensory abilities, enhancing your inner knowing, and developing introspection.

Mongoose Learning how to defend yourself swiftly, bravery, courage, fearlessness, possessing the ability to handle all situations, protection, and lacking fear.

Monkey   Learning how to honor ancestral ties and potential, working together in groups, possessing the ability to change focus, and success.

Moose   Teaching self-esteem, encouraging self-achievement and reward, going at unseen speed, achieving victory, brimming with enthusiasm, supporting personal talent and skills, and developing personal potential.

Mosquito   Honing in on your goals, driving your enemies crazy by continual pestering and nagging, moving in one direction, fertility, adaptability, and endurance.

Moth   Encouraging out-of-body experience, exploring other dimensions, dreaming, using psychic ability, knowing through intuition, possessing the ability to confuse enemies, finding light in the darkness, and developing shamanic talents.

Mouse   Teaching humility, paying attention to the small details of life, learning scrutiny in situations, learning to be unseen, taking action, developing concentration and focus, and doing one thing at a time.

Nightingale   Inspiring musical ability and creativity, representing the totem of performing artists, and learning rhythm in life.

Octopus   Learning versatility, developing many skills, juggling several tasks at once, moving away from difficulties, and developing your flexibility. To the Greeks and Minoans, the octopus symbolized the sacred spiral of the Goddess, representing the moon phases, feminine powers, and the cycle of life.

Opossum   Learning how to achieve your goals, using the ancient wisdom together with common sense, and climbing to ever-higher horizons.

Orangutan   Learning to communicate with nature, demonstrating ingenuity, staying ahead of problems, personal empowerment, and gentleness.

Ostrich   Learning how to examine and observe the world around you and how to size up situations and people, developing personal awareness, and overturning adverse situations.

Otter Balancing working and playing, maintaining invulnerability, keeping an open mind in unusual situations, and unmasking hidden talents. A reservoir of boundless energy, the otter is considered sacred and magical because it is vulnerable only in the spot beneath its chin and under its forearm.

Owl Learning discernment, knowing the difference between truth and deception, performing transformation, experiencing insights, working with ley lines (energy lines), developing intuitive skills, attuning to lunar cycles, moon magic, and gaining rapport with the Goddess. The owl is a sacred symbol of the Goddess.

Oxen Developing your intuition, inspiring divine inspiration, providing sacred energy, recognizing the spiritual in all things, and learning faithfulness.

Oyster Growth, wisdom, reward after seeing patterns through, self-responsibility, taking opportunities as they arise, persistence, and sensitivity to your environment.

Panda Developing methodical ability, performing scientific investigation, and working to unravel mysteries.

Panther Embracing the unknown, leaping ahead and overcoming the fear of the dark, confronting unseen fears and enemies, learning self-trust, taking time to discover the truth, and reclaiming your personal power.

Parrot Developing personal skills by mimicking and imitating others, serving an apprenticeship, practicing and refining skills, learning to think before speaking, and bringing rain.

Peacock Magic power, protection, strutting your potential, developing visual skills, seeing the world through your mind's eye, psychic ability, intuition, clairvoyance, telepathy, immortality, self-confidence, and divine inspiration and guidance.

Pegasus Immortality, reincarnation, renewal, eternal evolution of nature, spiritual knowing, and facing life head-on.

Pelican Gaining abundance, controlling your ego, participating in renewal and recovery, and tapping into the Earth's knowledge.

Penguin Developing unity, working together in groups as one, connecting to nature, learning how to become part of a unified group, exhibiting patience, becoming adaptable, and committing to a cause.

Pheasant Recognizing your achievements and abilities, satisfying your needs, changing negative habits, blending with your environment, and concealing secrets.

Phoenix A magical creature of rebirth and healing. Cultivating the ability to appear and disappear at will, Sun energy and solar power, regeneration, rejuvenation, resurrection, healing, renewal, loyalty, and service. Appearing as an oversized red swan, the phoenix has tears with remarkable healing powers. Phoenix is the Greek name for the fabled Egyptian Bennu bird, which was the symbol of the Sun.

Pig Learning the proper use of your mind, using knowledge wisely, and discovering how to formulate opinions and think clearly.

Pigeon Teaches you the value of direction in life, instructs you how to set reasonable goals, assists you in navigational skills, and shows you how to get home.

Platypus Tapping into ancient Earth knowledge and wisdom, seeing things in a different way, relating to the world in new and innovative ways, and staying true to yourself.

Porcupine Regaining childlike innocence, learning to be a quiet observer, practicing noninterference, sticking to your personal patterns, and keeping your faith in someone.

Prairie Dog Learning the meaning and value of family and community, attuning with the seasons and nature, and being able to avoid dangerous situations.

Praying Mantis Learning the proper use of prayer to change consciousness, ridding your life of negativity, protecting your immediate environment, heightening your awareness, manipulating time, acquiring the power of stillness, and learning strategies for survival.

Python Brings beneficial changes, good luck, new ideas, windfall, and inheritance.

Quail Teaching you how to use economy in everyday activities, using only what you need, and working in harmony with others.

Raccoon Offering protection, learning how to provide for yourself and your family, developing your ability to share with others, developing dexterity, using disguises, and curiosity.

Rat   Providing fertility, inspiring renewal, learning to escape and defend yourself in tight corners, and developing cunning and intelligence.

Raven   Developing magical ability, divination, omens, messages from nature, forewarning of danger, learning to trust your intuition, new insights, and exploring the unknown. The Druids divined the future by watching the behavior of ravens. The raven is a symbol of magic and sorcery.

Rhinoceros   Taking charge of situations and pushing ventures forward, going it alone, moving ahead, not giving up, even in difficult situations, and trusting your instincts.

Robin   Teaches you how to parent children and nurture others and how to caretake nature and living things, learning how to share with others, taking care of pets, sticking to your patterns, and understanding the power of song.

Rolly Polly Bug   Learning how to roll with the punches, learning flexibility and how to flow with events, applying constant effort toward goals and personal objectives, and working from the ground up.

Salamander   Teaching how to use passion for creativity, developing personal energy, igniting thoughts and ideas, and helping to discover hidden talents. In magic, the salamander sometimes appears as a tiny, brilliant white-gold lizard that feeds on fire flames.

Salmon   A symbol of renewal, sustenance, abundance, teaching wisdom and inner knowing, improving memory, healing inner voices, regeneration, fertility, returning home, prophecy, and divination. In Celtic mythology, it is said that all that has ever happened is retained in the salmon's memory.

Scorpion   Providing powers of death and rebirth, sending negativity back to its sender, knowing how to defend yourself, enabling transmutation, and developing psychic abilities.

Sea Lion (Seal)   Developing your intuition and learning how to trust your hunches and gut reactions, accepting your inner signals, and becoming more playful and charming.

Seagull Moving beyond your imagination, learning to go with the flow, taking opportunities as soon as they are presented, understanding spiritual messages, and working together in group situations.

Selkie Using shapeshifting, communicating with ancestors, understanding the powers of the sea, exhibiting flexibility, showing loyalty, enabling transformation. The Selkie transforms, via its sealskin, from a person to a seal, and back again.

Shark Learning how not to be caught off guard, being able to defend yourself, developing freedom of movement, and heightening sense of smell.

Sheep Fertility, inspiring new beginnings, maintaining balance in emergency and crises, gaining confidence, and creating abundance.

Skunk Encouraging solitary development of your magical abilities, and attracting unusual people and situations into your life.

Sloth Learning the value of moving slowly, attuning with tree energy, approaching your goals methodically, and switching perspectives and seeing both sides of the coin.

Snake Learning how to shed outworn habits, acquaintances, lovers, and places, letting go of the past, possessing immortality, fertility and sensuality, learning elusiveness, enabling transmutation, accepting and welcoming change, divination, creative energy, and psychic development. The snake is seen in druidism as the symbol of the life force that runs or "snakes" through both the land and each of us.

Sparrow Developing skills of sudden and quick movement and thought, discovering the power of song, boundless energy, fertility, sexuality, increased desire, and natural instinct.

Sphinx Learning to speak in riddles, questioning your world, strength, endurance, and guarding treasure and heritage. The Sphinx appears as a gigantic human-headed lion.

Spider Weaving the patterns and people you chose into your life, creating and constructing your personal web of life, developing your dreaming skills, and learning to follow your bliss—that which you truly love.

Squirrel Using your resources appropriately, saving for a rainy day, developing a more playful nature, increasing intelligence, and performing quick movement.

Stag Positive male energy; support; Goddess magic; fertility; tapping into the ancient wisdom of lineages; using the power of ley lines, love magic, forest magic, and ancestral communication; and honoring Earth.

Starfish Developing magical abilities, connecting with the stars and celestial bodies, attuning with lunar and tidal rhythms, and regenerating.

Starling Imitation, adaptability, mental receptivity, and ability to calm large groups of people.

Swallow Swooping down on your enemies or diving into a project, learning how to work together in communities, knowing when thunderstorms will occur, possessing ability to outmaneuver your opponents, and attuning with seasonal cycles.

Swan Discovering your inner mate, developing personal grace and sensitivity, eloquence, and nobility, moving beyond family patterns, divination, clairvoyant dreams, awakening your personal power, finding your life mate, and transforming gracefully. Killing a swan brings great misfortune.

Tasmanian Devil Protecting your territory, knowing when to fight your opponent, and using self-defense.

Tiger Gaining power, strength, and a surplus of energy, demonstrating willpower, and using swift instinctual action without intellectual analysis.

Toad Holding your ground, speaking up when you feel strongly about an issue, repelling negativity, changing your luck, longevity, and protection.

Turkey Learning how to give generously to others, letting go of the past, and moving out of harm's way.

Turtle Providing service, learning to give, teaching you how to work in rapport with the Earth and the Goddess, fertility, abundance, and forgiveness, understanding, ancestral communication, the step-by-step "slow but sure" way to accomplish your goals, developing navigational skills, self-reliance, protection, and tenacity. Turtle Island is the ancient name for North America.

Unicorn   Acknowledging beauty, love, and friendship, learning the gentle side of life, developing magical and psychic abilities, acquiring occult wisdom, and experiencing multidimensional travel and awareness. The unicorn appears as a magical white horse with one horn.

Vulture   Learning to recycle ideas, feelings, and other aspects of your life, your crone face, full moon wisdom, death and rebirth, prophecy, purification, patience, letting go of outworn habits and friendships, and primordial energy.

Walrus   Developing social and business skills, learning how to come out ahead, discovering the path with the least resistance, getting your life flowing again, abundance, prosperity, money, wealth, making wise investments, and creativity.

Warthog   Developing ability to sense danger, protecting, learning how to defend yourself, and discovering the truth.

Weasel   Teaching you how to escape difficult situations, sharpening intelligence, learning how to be a natural detective, using keen observation, and noticing the little signs and signals all around you every moment.

Whale   Sounding board, the song of life, personal destiny, and discovering your personal path. The whale is the record keeper of the Earth, helpful in developing dignity, kindness, and psychic and unusual forms of tonal communication.

Wolf   Providing protection and security, developing your sense of smell, using your inner and primal knowing, loyalty to family, friendship, steadfastness, guidance in dreams, discovering new ways of doing things, learning endurance and the art of invisibility, and moving beyond socially accepted constraints.

Wolverine Providing protection from opponents and those who mean to do you harm, giving spiritual protection, learning to be ferocious if necessary, using aggression to your benefit, and standing your ground.

Wren Moving quickly and deftly, understanding divine messages and signals, prophecy and divination, and attuning with the seasonal cycles.

Zebra Seeing things as black and white, finding your personal path, maintaining your individuality, and using personal empowerment.

BIBLIOGRAPHY

Adler, Margot. *Drawing Down the Moon*. Boston: Beacon Press, 1981.

Beyerl, Paul. *A Compendium of Herbal Magik*. Custer, Wash.: Phoenix Publishing, 1998.

Brennan, Barbara Ann. *Light Emerging*. New York: Bantam Books, 1993.

Bryant, Page. *Starwalking: Shamanic Practices for Traveling into the Night Sky*. Santa Fe, N.M.: Bear and Company, 1997.

Buckland, Raymond. *Wicca for Life*. New York: Kensington Publishing, 2001.

Buhlman, William. *Adventures Beyond the Body*. San Francisco: Harper San Francisco, 1996.

Canfield, Jack, Mark Victor Hansen, and Les Hewitt. *The Power of Focus*. Deerfield Beach, Fla.: Health Communications, 2000.

Coffey, Lisa Marie. *Getting There with Grace*. Boston, Mass.: Journey Editions, 2001.

Cunningham, Scott. *The Complete Book of Incense, Oils, and Brews*. St. Paul, Minn.: Llewellyn Publications, 1989.

———. *Encyclopedia of Magical Herbs*. St. Paul, Minn.: Llewellyn Publications, 1985.

Farrar, Janet and Stewart Farrar. *A Witches' Bible Compleat*. New York: Magickal Childe, 1984.

Gannon, Linda. *Creating Fairy Garden Fragrances*. Pownal, Vt.: Storey Books, 1998.

Garrett, Michael, and J. T. Garrett. *Medicine of the Cherokee*. Santa Fe, N.M.: Bear and Company, 1996.

Gawain, Shakti. *Creative Visualization*. Mill Valley, Calif.: Whatever Publishing, 1978.

Gimbutas, Marija. *The Language of the Goddess*. San Francisco: Harper & Row, 1989.

Godwin, Malcolm. *The Lucid Dreamer*. New York: Simon & Schuster, 1994.

Gray, Deborah. *The Good Witch's Guide to Wicked Ways*. Boston: Journey Editions, 2001.

Hathaway, Nancy. *The Friendly Guide to the Universe*. New York: Penguin Books, 1995.

Hay, Louise. *You Can Heal Your Life*. Carson, Calif.: Hay House, 1984.

Knight, Sirona. *Celtic Traditions*. New York: Citadel Press, 2000.

————. *Dream Magic: Night Spells and Rituals for Love, Prosperity, and Personal Power*. San Francisco: HarperSanFrancisco, 2000.

————. *Empowering Your Life with Dreams*. New York: Alpha Books, 2004.

————. *Empowering Your Life with Natural Magic*. New York: Alpha Books, 2004.

————. *Empowering Your Life with Wicca*. New York: Alpha Books, 2003.

————. *Exploring Celtic Druidism*. Franklin Lakes, N.J.: New Page Books, 2001.

————. *Faery Magick*. Franklin Lakes, N.J.: New Page Books, 2002.

————. *Goddess Bless!* Boston: Red Wheel, 2002.

————. *Greenfire: Making Love with the Goddess*. St. Paul, Minn.: Llewellyn Publications, 1995.

————. *The Little Giant Encyclopedia of Runes*. New York: Sterling Publishing, 2000.

————. *Love, Sex, and Magick*. New York: Citadel Press, 1999.

————. *Moonflower: Erotic Dreaming with the Goddess*. St. Paul, Minn.: Llewellyn Publications, 1996.

————. *The Pocket Guide to Crystals and Gemstones*. Freedom, Calif.: Crossing Press, 1998.

————. *The Wiccan Spell Kit*. New York: Citadel Press, 2001.

————. *The Witch and Wizard Training Guide*. New York: Citadel Press, 2001.

————, and D. J. Conway. *The Shapeshifter Tarot*. St. Paul, Minn.: Llewellyn Publications, 1998.

Leach, Maria, ed. *Standard Dictionary of Folklore, Mythology, and Legend*. New York: Funk & Wagnalls, 1950.

MacDonald, Lucy. *Learn to Be an Optimist*. San Francisco: Chronicle Books, 2004.

Monaghan, Patricia. *The Book of Goddesses and Heroines*. St. Paul, Minn.: Llewellyn Publications, 1990.

Morrison, Dorothy. *Everyday Magic*. St. Paul, Minn.: Llewellyn Publications, 1998.

Oman, Maggie, ed. *Prayers for Healing*. Berkeley, Calif.: Conari Press, 1997.

Rector-Page, Linda. *Healthy Healing*. Sonoma, Calif.: Healthy Healing Publications, 1992.

Rowling, J. K. *Harry Potter and the Chamber of Secrets*. New York: Scholastic, 1999.

———— *Harry Potter and the Goblet of Fire*. New York: Scholastic, 2000.

————*Harry Potter and the Prisoner of Azkaban*. New York: Scholastic, 1999.

————*Harry Potter and the Sorcerer's Stone*. New York: Scholastic, 1997.

Sabrina, Lady. *The Witch's Master Grimoire*. Franklin Lakes, N.J.: New Page Books, 2001.

Sams, Jamie. *Animal Medicine: A Guide to Claiming Your Spirit Allies*. Boulder, Colo.: Sounds True, 1996.

Schiller, David, and Carol Schiller. *Aromatherapy Basics*. New York: Sterling Publishing Co., 1998.

Scully, Nicki. *Power Animal Meditations*. Rochester, Vt.: Bear & Company, 2001.

Skafte, Dianne. *Listening to the Oracle*. New York: HarperSanFrancisco, 1997.

Starhawk. *The Spiral Dance*. San Francisco: HarperSanFrancisco, 1979.

Tolkien, J. R. R. *Tree and Leaf*. Boston: Houghton Mifflin, 1965.

Tuitean, Paul, and Estelle Daniels. *Pocket Guide to Wicca*. Freedom, Calif.: Crossing Press, 1998.

Weinstein, Marion. *Earth Magic*. New York: Earth Magic Productions, 1998.

Wesselman, Hank. *Medicinemaker: Mystic Encounters on the Shaman's Path*. New York: Bantam Books, 1998.

Williams, David, and Kate West. *Born in Albion*. Cheshire, England: Pagan Media, 1996.

Worwood, Valerie. *The Complete Book of Essential Oils and Aromatherapy*. New York: New World Library, 1995.